The origins of
Lancashire

The origins of
Lancashire

Denise Kenyon

Manchester University Press
Manchester and New York
Distributed exclusively in the USA and Canada by St. Martin's Press

Copyright © Denise Kenyon 1991

Published by Manchester University Press
Oxford Road, Manchester M13 9PL, England
and Room 400, 175 Fifth Avenue, New York, NY 10010, USA

Distributed exclusively in the USA and Canada
by St. Martin's Press, Inc., 175 Fifth Avenue, New York,
NY 10010, USA

British Library cataloguing in publication data
Kenyon, Denise
   The origins of Lancashire. – (Origins of the shire).
   1. Lancashire, to 1066
   I. Title   II. Series
   942.7601

Library of Congress cataloging in publication data
Kenyon, Denise, 1952–
      The origins of Lancashire/Denise Kenyon.
         p.   cm. – (Origins of the Shire)
      Includes index.
      IGBN 0–7190–3277–6. – ISBN 0–7190–3546–5 (pbk.)
      1. Lancashire (England) – History.   I. Title.   II. Series.
   DAB70. L2K48 1991
   942.7′6–dc20   90-25569

ISBN   0 7190 3277 6 *hardback*
       0 7190 3546 5 *paperback*

Phototypeset in Hong Kong by Best-set Typesetter Limited.
Printed in Great Britain by
Bell and Bain Ltd., Glasgow

Contents

Contents

Figures and plates

Figures

Note: Township boundaries have been taken from the Lancashire County Record Office map of pre-1888 townships.

Plates

Plates appear between pages 108 and 109

General Editor's preface

The shire was the most important single unit of government, justice and social organisation throughout the Later Middle Ages and on into the Modern period. An understanding of the shire is, therefore, fundamental to English history of all sorts and of all periods – be it conducted on a national, regional or local basis.

This series sets out to explore the origins of each shire in the Early Middle Ages. Archaeological evidence for settlement hierarchies and social territories in later prehistory and the Roman period is necessarily the starting-point. The shire and its component parts are then explored in detail during the Anglo-Saxon period. A series of leading scholars with a particular regional expertise have brought together evidence drawn from literary and documentary sources, place-name research and archaeological fieldwork to present a stimulating picture of the territorial history of the English shires, and the parishes, estates and hundreds of which they were formed.

In some instances the results stress the degree of continuity across periods as long as a millennium. Elsewhere, these studies underline the arbitrary nature of the shire and the intentional break with the past, particularly where the West Saxon King, Edward the Elder, imposed his southern ideas concerning local organisation on the regional communities of the English Midlands.

These volumes will each be a great asset to historians and all those interested in their own localities, offering an open door into a period of the past which has, up to now, for many, been too difficult or obscure to attempt an entry.

Nick Higham

Acknowledgements

I would like to thank everyone who has helped in the writing and production of this volume. Particular thanks go to the series editor, Nick Higham, as well as to my family for their forbearance. For help with the index I am indebted to C. V. Horie.

This book has arisen partly out of the studies I made for my doctoral thesis at Manchester University, and partly out of Extra-Mural and WEA classes. It seems fitting that I should also record my gratitude to fellow postgraduates and colleagues, and to all of those class members whose enthusiasm has sustained me.

Abbreviations

BAR	British Archaeological Reports
HE	Bede's *Historia Ecclesiastica*, ed. C. Plummer, Oxford University Press, 1966
OE	Old English
ON	Old Norse
Scand.	Scandinavian
VCH	*The Victoria History of the County of Lancaster*, ed. W. Farrer *et al.*, Constable, 1906–14

Note

AD, BC	dates expressed in calendar years
ad, bc	dates expressed in radiocarbon years, uncalibrated
bp	date before present (1950) expressed in radiocarbon years, uncalibrated

1

Environment and land-use

Lancashire today is a much emasculated version of the medieval shire. The Mersey no longer marks its southern boundary; Lancaster no longer has a pivotal role for administering Furness and Cartmel North of the Sands. The county has lost the industrial and commercial centres of Manchester and Liverpool: these became the nuclei of metropolitan counties in 1974 (Fig. 1.1). Warrington was lost to Cheshire and the area North of the Sands was absorbed within the new county of Cumbria. In return, modern Lancashire has gained the Craven district of the former West Riding of Yorkshire and so all of Bowland Forest now lies within its confines. These administrative changes of the 1970s have radically altered the nature of the shire, removing at the stroke of a pen several important pieces of its history and distorting its historical and geographical *raisons d'être*.

Physical background: geology and drift deposits

'Lancastria' has long been recognised by geographers as a discrete, unified region delimited by the carboniferous scarp which runs from Newcastle-under-Lyme through Rossendale and Bowland Forest up into the Lake District (Johnson 1985; King 1976). The scarp fixes the upland–lowland transition zone around 183 m. Today the scarp is marked by an arc of west-facing escarpments lying to the east of the main fault line. These escarpments include

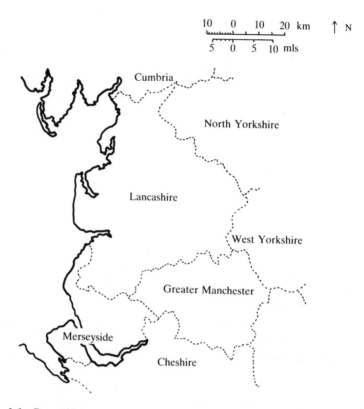

Fig. 1.1 Post-1974 administrative counties in the North-West

The boundaries of the historic counties were re-drawn to create the metropolitan counties of Greater Manchester and Merseyside, and the new
shire county of Lancashire

Horwich and Billinge Hill which lie just off the main line, and,
continuing northwards, Chorley, Longridge Fell, Calder Fell, Lee
Fell (Quernmore) and Furness Fell. The arc is less pronounced
in Lancashire just beyond the Lune, for the escarpments lie further inland from the county boundary, near Kirkby Lonsdale.
This high land roughly marks the edge of the county to the north
and east, the sea of Morecambe Bay marks the western side, and
the Mersey functioned as Lancashire's southern boundary. Within
the confines of the ancient county the diversity of landscape is
striking. From the limestone crags and caves in Lancashire North

of the Sands, the barren expanses of peat-covered millstone grits, shales and coal measures of Rossendale Forest, to the almost lunar landscape of sand dunes at Ainsdale and Birkdale, it is a county of contrasts. Frequently the county is subdivided into topographical units like the Fylde Plain and the Rossendale Uplands, which are used as both landscape and agricultural land-use categories (Rodgers 1955).

The carboniferous scarp is the most distinctive feature in Lancashire and it is clear that the characteristics of the uplands in Lancashire are strongly dependent on the underlying rock formations and structures as modified by glacial action. Indeed, the present drainage pattern of the major rivers largely reflects structural elements. The major rivers run broadly from east to west, draining the uplands into Morecambe Bay. From the north, in a clockwise direction, they are the Duddon, Leven, Kent, Lune, Wyre, Ribble (plus its tributaries the Calder and Hodder), the Douglas which runs into the sea at the Ribble estuary, and the Mersey with its tributaries, especially the Irwell (Fig. 1.2). Extensive lowland mosses flank several of these rivers and their estuaries. Lancashire North of the Sands lies on the southern fringe of the Lake District. The bed of England's largest lake, Lake Windermere, was not actually in Lancashire for the county boundary used to run along its shoreline. Coniston, the scene of water speed records, lay entirely within Lancashire. Here is found some of the best-known scenery in the whole country, made famous by Wordsworth and Ruskin. Both had strong ties with the area: John Ruskin had a house on the shore of Coniston Water; Wordsworth was educated at Hawkshead. The oldest rocks in the county are to be found here. These are the Ordovician rocks of the Borrowdale volcanic series which begin around Windermere and Coniston and form the centre of the Lake District. To the south are the younger Silurian rocks of High Furness. Younger still are the carboniferous limestone outcrops which occur widely between the 200 m and 300 m contours, especially around the northern shores of Morecambe Bay, as at Warton Crag, for example. Caves are common in the limestone. The older ones are found around the Bay where they have frequently developed close to the sea. A particularly good example can be seen on the western side of Humphrey Head just outside Grange-Over-Sands. Younger ones have formed up the Lune valley, on Leck Fell, for

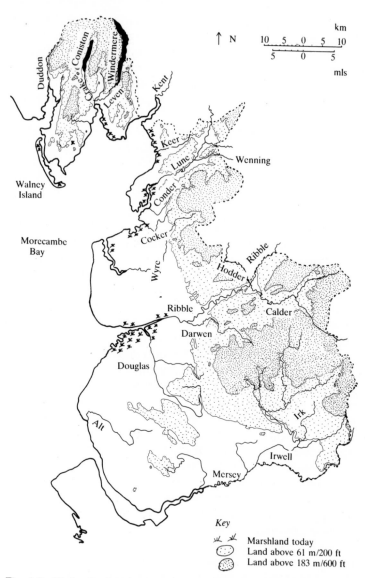

Fig. 1.2 Main physical features in Lancashire

example, where one can discover caves with associated tunnels and passages.

In the uplands of the Forests of Bowland and Pendle the limetones are interbedded with shales and sandstones. Outcrops of limestone are rather uncommon and are restricted to the Clitheroe area (Pl. 2). Blanket peat begins to appear between 200 m and 300 m and the slopes are free of drift material above 430 m. Not surprisingly, farmsteads are rare above 250 m. One principal landscape feature of the hills behind Lancaster is the Trough of Bowland, a meltwater channel which cuts across the main watershed. The Trough, which lies in an Area of Outstanding Natural Beauty (AONB), is a favourite Sunday afternoon drive for many people (Brodie 1990), affording spectacular views from the moors right across to Blackpool Tower and the Morecambe Bay coastline. A more important communication corridor is the Ribble–Aire Gap. This gap, which lies between Bowland and Pendle, links the valley of the Ribble and its tributaries with the valley of the Aire on the east of the Pennines. Settlements and archaeological finds along the route, ranging from Bronze Age axes to Viking silver, indicate its long-standing importance. Numerous drumlins (deposits of glacial till) spread down the Ribble valley where they have sometimes been wrongly identified as prehistoric tumuli. Drumlins are fairly common across much of north Lancashire, especially to the north of the Wyre towards Lancaster, and in Furness. These drumlins range from 75 m to 1,600 m long and can be as much as 150 m high. They were favoured spots for early settlements, acting as islands of higher land above the poorly-drained soils found in many townships.

Further south are the broad, flattened plateaux of Rossendale Forest. Prominent amongst the carboniferous rocks here are coal measures and the millstone grits proper, hard gritstone bands separated by softer shales. It is the differential erosion of these grits and shales which has produced the characteristic stepped profiles of the Rossendale Moors. Locally the millstone grits were an important building material, typically used for the small terraced rows built to house mill workers in the Pennine valleys. As with Bowland Forest, there has been glacial modification of these uplands. The action of meltwaters is important here too, and glacial valleys continue to fulfil communication needs, as for instance Walsden Gorge, used successively by the Turnpike Road of 1760 (A6033), Rochdale Canal at the turn of the century, and by the Manchester–Leeds Railway in 1840. The higher plateaux above about 300 m are now covered by extensive deposits of blanket peat. This peat is typically between 1 m and 2 m in depth though it can reach 4 m or 5 m in depressions. The amount of current peat formation is debatable since the optimum conditions for growth, rainfall of at least 1,000 mm and cool summers, are rarely achieved except on the top of the moorland plateaux. Drift deposits cover most of the lower slopes and fells flanking the carboniferous scarp. The lower slopes of Rossendale Forest are covered by Pennine Drift above about 60–90 m. This is also the predominant drift material on the foothills of the Forests of Bowland and Pendle. A slightly different material, Lake District Drift, is found on Furness and Cartmel Fells.

The Lancashire Plain, which includes the Fylde and south-west Lancashire, is approximately delimited by the 100–120 m contours. The underlying rocks are mostly Triassic. Some earlier coal measures are exposed north-east of Liverpool and they form the basis of the South Lancashire Coalfield in the triangle bounded by Skelmersdale, Colne and Oldham. Sometimes the coal measures reach thicknesses of over 1,000 m, as they do in the Manchester embayment where 1,420 m is reached. They are only about half of this thickness in the Wigan area. Drift cover is patchy in south-west Lancashire and sandstone outcrops occur in several places, including Melling, Ince Blundell, Haskayne, Barton (south-west Lancashire) and Thornton. Outcrops of carboniferous rocks tend to form the highest ground, as for example at Billinge Hill (179 m) and Parbold (153 m). In the Fylde rock outcrops are rare; there has been considerable erosion of the underlying rocks and there is a deep drift layer. Generally the plain is covered by Northern Drift which was deposited by the Irish Sea. Northern Drift extends from the Fylde down the south-west Lancashire corridor into west and central Cheshire. It forms a rough cresent in the Fylde where it covers the Fylde Ridge. The Ridge is in fact a discontinuous multiple ridge running from Blackpool through Kirkham towards the edge of Bowland Forest. The drift, which can reach a thickness of up to 45 m, is mostly till with some interleaved layers of sand and gravel. The pattern of deposition is fairly consistent across the plain but there is much debate about its precise origin. In particular, questions have been raised concerning whether the interleaved sands and gravels resulted from one complex deposition phase or whether two or more distinct glacial advances are involved. On balance, current opinion favours the former viewpoint. Northern Drift is a reddish-brown slightly stony material and it is slightly calcareous. According to Sobee (1953), men were paid a penny (pre-decimal coinage; presumably this was in the late nineteenth or early twentieth century) each for digging out holes in the clay under the peat at Pilling. This clay was used as fertiliser. These 'penny holes' can be compared with the marl pits of Cheshire; in both cases calcareous deposits were extracted for agricultural use.

Most of these complicated glacial deposits were laid down during and after the major glacial period of between 20,000 and 16,000 years ago. In the subsequent period terraces along the major rivers, especially the Lune, Ribble and Mersey, were formed. The last of the ice retreated from the North-West around 10,000 years ago. In the immediate post-glacial period the coastline lay far to the west of the present-day one. As the ice sheets thawed global sea-levels rose and there was a progressive eastward migration of the Lancashire coastline. At one time it was thought that the line of low cliffs identified by Gresswell (1953) at the 17 ft (5·18 m) contour line from Hesketh Bank to Shirdley Hill in south-west Lancashire (the so-called Hillhouse Coast, named after the cliff at the edge of Altcar Moss) corresponded with the 25 ft raised beach in Scotland, and marked the line of the coast around 5,000 BC. It is now realised that the Hillhouse Coast does not have a marine origin. In the Downholland area it represents the former lake shore or edge of the lake at Martin Mere (Tooley 1978).

The principal post-glacial superficial deposits are alluvium, especially important around the coast and river mouths, peat and blown sand. Drying in late and post-glacial times caused redeposition of sand over an area of more than 200 sq km of the south-west Lancashire coastal plain. This sand, called Shirdley Hill Sand, is an invaluable raw material and explains the location of the glass manufacturing industry at St Helens. Recent blown sand is also found along the coast at Walney Island, near Fleetwood, and from Southport to Crosby where it now forms extensive dunes. New dunes were being formed near Southport in the 1830s and the rate of dune formation has increased significantly since then. At Ainsdale the dune belt is 4 km wide. Deliberate efforts are now made to stabilise the dunes by promoting the growth of marram grass. The dunes at Ainsdale are one of the few remaining haunts of the natterjack toad (*Bufo calamita*), the only British amphibian favoured with legal protection.

Peat formation is another feature of the last 10,000 years. The extensive peat deposits occurring on upland moors above about 300 m have already been mentioned and the oldest blanket peat on Rossendale is thought to be over 6,000 years old. Upland peat growth is heavily dependent on climatic factors, but it is thought that the actual origins of this blanket peat owes much to the activities of man. Before the Bronze Age these moors were often covered with woodland vegetation – the tree line in fact lies at 640 m in Scotland and is unlikely to be lower in this part of England. Successive clearance phases denuded the upland slopes, rendering them vulnerable to the effects of erosion. The removal of the tree cover also affected the surface drainage, and because of the disruption in the ecological cycle leaf litter was no longer available as a source of organic matter for the soil. Soils became progressively thinner and more acidic which in turn precluded woodland generation. By about 3,000 years ago peat deposits had begun to form over an extensive area. Today the survival of this upland peat is threatened by erosion, sheep grazing, air pollution and artificial drainage schemes.

Peat deposits in the lowlands are often referred to as mosslands. Medieval documents use the Latin term *mossa* and the word moss-land became popular after the late eighteenth century, following the publication of Yates's map of 1786. Mosses are characterised by the presence of the plant bog moss or *sphagnum*, which decays to form slightly raised peat bogs. Poor surface drainage conditions are a major factor in the growth of these lowland deposits; the cloudy weather so often experienced in western Lancashire is a contributory factor since this reduces evaporation. Peat has developed in kettle holes left after the last glaciation as at Marton Mere in the Fylde. The dyke draining the mere, called Spen Dyke in 1730, is the original 'pool' of Blackpool. Peat constituted an important natural resource in earlier times. Peat from Pilling and Cockerham Mosses was used as fuel for the salt industry which had developed by the Tudor period to exploit the deposits of rock salt at Preesall. Peat was cut, dried and then used for fuel. Rights of turbary (peat cutting) are frequently listed along with other common rights in medieval documents.

The oldest moss in the county is probably Chat Moss, flanking the lower reaches of the Mersey, which originated at the end of the glacial period. Its major period of growth occurred around 7,000 years ago. By contrast the mosses along the Alt and Douglas and in the Pilling area are only about 4,000 years old. Mosses in the Fylde itself and the west Lune group are more recent, perhaps only 1,500 to 2,000 years old. Their main period of growth is therefore post-Roman and these mosses are believed to seal important evidence for former settlements. Field walking and aerial surveys have only a limited value for mossland areas, but archaeological survey work using remote sensing techniques is becoming increasingly sophisticated, and holds out great promise for future archaeological investigation in the North-West.

Settlement and land-use potential

Lowland mosses occupied considerable acreages in former times, especially in south-west Lancashire. As early maps show, it was often difficult to decide where land ended and the sea began because of this coastal moss and dune belt zone. It was particulary difficult in the area around Downholland Moss. Martin Mere is now all that has survived of a freshwater lake there which was once 6 km long and which covered an area of 687 ha. Drainage of these mosses has taken place on a piecemeal basis from at least medieval times. The many references in Burscough Cartulary to ditch-enclosed fields reflect the practice of enclosing land on the periphery of Downholland Moss and using the ditches for drainage purposes. Thirteenth-century dykes are also mentioned near the Black Lake, 'a terrible black morass' at Pilling Moss. The Cartulary of Cockersand Abbey contains many references to thirteenth-century 'sykes' and ditched land throughout the Fylde. Efforts were made during the seventeenth and eighteenth centuries to effect large-scale drainage, but with little long-term success. The scheme at Halsall was typical of the period: attempts were made to drain land newly enclosed from the Downholland Moss complex in the 1750s, but problems with persistent flooding from the remaining open water of Martin Mere caused the abandonment of most of the reclaimed land. Initially, the drainage of Chat Moss was not much more successful. The third Duke of Bridgewater began reclamation in 1758, but by 1773 a large area had reverted to pasture. Nineteenth-century efforts had more success and the Liverpool–Manchester Railway, constructed between 1820 and 1830, ran across the moss. By 1849 around 800 ha had been reclaimed but this still left about two-thirds of the moss as unreclaimed 'waste'. The agricultural survey of the country of 1850–51 noted that two-thirds of the Fylde was also undrained and relatively unimproved (Caird 1968). In Lancashire as a whole the major phase of reclamation was between 1845 and 1880, and was principally due to the increased demand for agricultural produce on the part of the huge populations flooding into the industrial centres of south-east Lancashire.

Drainage and reclamation has continued into the second half of the twentieth century and today it is estimated that under 1,000 ha of mossland are left as grazing moss, scrub, etc. Most of this lies north of the Wyre and around the lower reaches of the Duddon and Leven. Few mosses retain anything of their original character. Centuries of peat-cutting, drainage and reclamation have destroyed wildlife habitats on an enormous scale. Winmarleigh Moss, a Site of Special Scientific Interest (SSSI), is the last remaining extensive area (60 ha) of raised bog on the Lancashire Plain. The RSPB reserve at Silverdale and the Wildfowl and Wetlands Trust's reserve at Martin Mere (near Burscough) represent a tiny fraction of the parent mosses. Conservationists are attempting to reclaim parts of other mosses and to restore their wetland ecology. At Risley Moss, near Warrington, the water level dropped considerably between 1800 and 1930 owing to drainage and large-scale peat-cutting. The water level was raised by around 6 ft in the 1970s and there is now a popular Nature Park on the site.

Once reclaimed and given the treatment available to modern farmers – mechanised drainage construction, chemical fertilisers, etc., these former mossland soils are now amongst the most fertile in the whole country. These reclaimed peat soils have the highest agricultural land-use classification grades (class 1), and are famous for the raising of crops like Blackpool tomatoes (Fylde mosses). Yet in the medieval period these very same soils would have fallen into the lowest category of soils (class 6) if classified according to their land-use capability. Generally speaking most Lancashire soils are only moderately suitable for agricultural use according to modern definitions. On the range from 1 to 6 most soils fall into classes 3 and 4. The Land Utilisation Survey of 1941 found that Lancashire had a larger percentage of poor quality land than was average for England as a whole (Smith 1941; Stamp 1962). The contrast with nearby Cheshire is striking: in that county 79 per cent was classed as good quality land, whereas the figure fell to 42 per cent in Lancashire.

Modern land-use maps have been produced as a guide to modern agricultural potential. They are less useful as a guide to former patterns of settlement and land-use and need supplementing with the maps produced by the Soil Survey (Hall and Folland 1970). As the soil maps show, gleyed soils predominate across the county. Most common are the surface-water gleys (stagnogleys) which are normally wet for significant periods of the year. They are less widespread than in Cheshire, though they still occur widely over much of the county, especially over much of the lowland plain and the Fylde, and on the slopes of the Forests of Bowland, Trawden, Pendle and Rossendale. Ground-water gleys tend to be saturated from below and are found extensively along river flood plains like the Wyre and at the Ribble estuary. Better drained and more fertile brown earths are occasionally found over fluvio-glacial deposits on the plain, and especially along river terrace deposits. They also occur on the upland fringes of the Lancashire Plain, especially on the flanks of Rossendale Forest. Brown earths predominate on the foothills of the Lake District, especially around Hawkshead and around the Morecambe Bay coast. Loamy brown rankers, the typical brown earth found over limestone, occur around Carnforth and Warton, and again at Clitheroe. Podzols, poor sandy soils with marked leaching of nutrients, are found where deciduous woodland has been replaced by conifers or heathers, on Longridge Fell, the Pennines and occasionally over sandstone protrusions on the plain. It is estimated that peat soils cover about one-tenth of the county. They occur sporadically across Lancashire, in enclosed hollows and along the edge of peat deposits. On the coastal plains they are particularly common along the River Douglas near Rufford and along stretches of the Wyre. Raw peat soils develop over former raised bogs under the influence of high ground-water levels. They are particularly noticeable at Rainford on Chat Moss, around Bolton, at Winmarleigh and Warton, and in the valleys of the Duddon and Leven in north Lancashire.

Soil forms in response to a variety of factors. In Lancashire the main soil-forming factors are parent material (usually drift), relief and drainage, and climate. External factors also play a role, such as the effects of man and the length of time since the soil began to be formed. It is estimated that mature podzols, for example, take between 1,500 and 3,000 years to develop. Very little new soil is still being formed today in England; the podzols developing along the Formby–Southport coastline are an exception. They have formed as a result of late nineteenth-century conifer planting and after seventy years or so their profiles show weakly developed soil horizons often only 2 cm thick.

Changes in land-use potential

As noted above, in practice, the amount of land available for agriculture and settlement in earlier times clearly depended very much not just on soil fertility characteristics, but also on drainage requirements and potential. At least 50 per cent of the soils in Lancashire are poorly drained. The agricultural exploitation of mossland areas in the medieval period, for example, was restricted to sheep grazing on Pilling Moss and at Rossall, not just because of the infertility of the peat soil, but also because they were so low-lying that they were susceptible to flooding. Large areas of west Lancashire lie below 7 m – an estimated 54 sq km in the Fylde and 148 sq km in south-west Lancashire. The highest recorded storm tides reach 7·6 m and much of this area would be regularly flooded were it not for an elaborate system of coastal defences and flood embankments. The last major flooding in the Martin Mere area in the 1950s prompted the Crossens scheme which has been designed to pump excess water into the sea. The exact area liable to flooding varies with the relative changes in sea-level. Tooley (1978) has studied the history of marine transgressions along the north-western coastline and has noted nine major episodes over the last 10,000 years or so, affecting a progressively smaller area as the river estuaries, etc., have changed and silted up. Low sea-levels occurred at the end of the fifth century BC, and again around the early seventh century AD. On three occasions in the last 3,000 years, however, sea-levels have been higher than present-day levels, around 2,650, 1,800 and 800 years ago (700 BC, and the third and twelfth centuries AD). The danger is particularly acute when coastal flooding affects the tidal limits of the rivers. This is at its worst when the incoming tide meets the run-off from the hills, hence the flood catchment basins constructed in recent years at Garstang. A related factor is the damage caused by sudden storm surges. Extensive coastal flooding was recorded in 1720, 1833, 1907 and 1927. Lancashire has a relatively long seaboard, extending from Plain Furness to the Mersey estuary, and the Bay experiences the second largest tidal range in Britain, second only to the Severn Bore, which itself is the largest in Europe. The standard tidal range in spring between low and high tide is 9·5 m. At other times it is around 6 m. The danger comes when a particularly low tide coincides with storms and fierce gales, when the most extreme tidal range can reach 11·5 m. In Morecambe Bay there are extensive sandbanks and shoals; beaches frequently exceed 1 km and at Southport and St Annes the sandy foreshore extends for 5 km. Exposed sand can be blown inland, causing widespread damage to crops, livestock and property. Nicholas Blundell's diary describes in detail the effect of one such storm surge on the south-west Lancashire coast on the night of 18–19 December 1720. 'There was a violent overflowing of the sea' which 'overflowed 6,600 Aikers of Land, and washed down 157 Houses and damnifyed 200 more' (Beck 1953). These floods affected areas both north and south of the Ribble estuary. The loss was not only of crops and livestock but at least nine lives. The mention in the Cartulary of Cockersand Abbey to the 'carrying of sand' may refer to the practice of mixing sand and peat to give more productive soil, or it could be a reference to some form of 'clean-up operation' after a storm.

Coastal erosion – and accretion – is a further problem. This is less obvious nowadays due to our extensive coastal defences. In former days land was lost to the sea on a significant scale, the loss at Blackpool before the 20 km-long defences were constructed has been calculated at as much as 2 m annually. Sea walls were built at Blackpool between 1895 and 1899, and had to be set back further in 1910 (Banks 1936). The coastal defences were then extended to Bispham where a major programme of cliff reinforcement has been implemented. The tip of Rossall Point was washed away, including the putative *Portus Setantiorum* of Roman times. Erosion has been noted at Sunderland Point near Heysham and at the site of Cockersand Abbey. Further south, erosion has affected a number of small coastal settlements. According to local tradition, the lost village of Singleton Thorpe which once stood to the west of Norbreck is now under the sea, as is the site of nearby Wadden Thorpe. Land in Kelgrymoles churchyard near St Annes was 'worne into the sea two or three miles', the Domesday vill of *Argarmeols* near Southport was 'drowned and adnichilate', and land on the west side of Walney island was lost according to pleas in the Duchy of Lancaster Courts in Tudor times (Fishwick 1898). Accretion is more difficult to trace in records, but has certainly been happening in recent times at the south-east tip of Walney Island, at Warton, Carnforth and at Pilling where there has been expansion of salt marshes, and along the coast south of Southport where the dune belt has progressively widened.

Settlement loss is not just a problem encountered in the lowest-lying areas of the county. It also affects the situation at the upper altitudinal margins. The Old Man of Coniston, 801 m high, is by far the highest spot in the county, but there is a considerable amount of land over 300 m. The highest parts of the Forest of Bowland exceed 550 m in Lancashire; heights of over 450 m are encountered in Rossendale. Today the bleak moorland plateaux of Rossendale up to around 385 m are dotted with abandoned farmsteads dating back to a brief period of expansion in the nineteenth century (Pl. 3). The local climate is both cooler and wetter the higher one climbs. The highest annual amounts of rainfall in the county are recorded around Coniston Water and Lake Windermere, where average annual values up to 2,400 mm were reached between 1941 and 1970. Average rainfall on Furness Fell and Bowland reaches 1,600 mm per year, Pendle and Rossendale exceed 1,200 mm though over 1,500 mm were recorded at Helmshore in the 1950s. These amounts are nearly double those experienced across lowland Lancashire. Temperatures vary significantly as well, and the lapse rate for Lancashire has been estimated at approximately 0·5 °C for every 70 m of height (Crowe 1962).

Obviously these figures are only guides to the actual rainfall and temperature levels, since local situations vary according to aspect and slope, but broadly speaking it means that there is a difference of around six or seven weeks in the growing season between the two extremes in Lancashire South of the Sands (Smith 1976; Bendelow and Hartnup 1980). The differences across the county are broadly from the far north-east to the south-west, in other words, it follows the distribution of high ground. The extremes are even more marked in Lancashire North of the Sands. It is worth mentioning that it is not only the growing season that is affected by climatic and altitudinal factors, but also the grazing season. Excessive soil wetness, not drought, is the usual problem in Lancashire. There is a serious risk of waterlogging, especially towards the end of the season, and so the upland grazing season is curtailed.

The altitudinal limits of settlement viability have fluctuated according to major shifts in the overall climate. In the past, there has been a tendency to think of our climate as a fixed part of our environment, as something that has remained basically unchanged since the Ice Age drew to a close over 10,000 years ago. It is now becoming increasingly widely recognised, however, that there have been periods of climatic change in our more recent past – indeed, we appear to be experiencing one during our own lifetime. These changes need not always involve dramatic changes in average temperatures or rainfall; in marginal areas such as the north-west of England, even small variations can have a significant impact on settlement and agriculture. Because of the effect of the altitudinal lapse rate, a fluctuation in average annual temperatures of as little as 0·5 °C can result in the extension or contraction of agriculture, and consequently of settlement, over a theoretical altitudinal range of 70 m in Lancashire. If the climate warms up by one degree, the altitudinal thresholds are raised by 140 m. The warming-up of the climate after the 'Mini Ice-Age' of the seventeenth century, when Frost Fairs were held on the Thames, led to the spread of farmsteads on the Rossendale plateaux. A similar situation occurred during the 'Little Climatic Optimum' of the medieval period. This period of climatic amelioration began around the middle years of the ninth century according to Lamb, reaching its peak around the twelfth and thirteenth centuries (Lamb 1977). At the other end of the country, on Dartmoor, deserted villages and farmsteads like Hound Tor bear mute testimony to this external colonisation movement (Austin, in Hooke 1985). A similar phenomenon occurred in Lancashire, though it is far less well represented in the archaeological record. It was probably during this period that upland pastures began to be fully exploited; temporary enclosures and sheiling sites were occupied on a more permanent footing.

This warmer period followed an appreciably cooler and/or wetter episode during which there was a renewal of growth of the Pennine peats. The date of this renewal of growth, marked in the deposit as a recurrence surface, is around AD 500, which ties in with periods of renewed growth from Rusland in Lancashire North of the Sands (Dickinson 1975), from Wessenden just across the county boundary from Oldham (Tallis 1964), and indeed elsewhere in northern Britain and Scandinavia (Aaby 1976). This recurrence surface is correlated with Granlund RY II, a widespread recurrence surface named after the man who first recognized its significance in Sweden. An earlier recurrence surface (identified with Granlund RY III) occurred before 500 BC and also marks a time when the climate was appreciably cooler and wetter than today. Growth horizons of this date have been noted in several deposits in and around Lancashire. The wooden trackway near Pilling known as Kates Pad (which has a radiocarbon age of around 810 ±bc) was constructed at the transition from drier to wetter conditions in the first part of the first millennium BC. These two recurrence surfaces are particulary important for dating purposes as they bracket the later prehistoric (Iron Age) and Roman periods in the North-West. Even if radiocarbon dates are not available for a peat profile, these periods of renewed growth, usually easily identifiable in the sections, give some useful termini. By reference to them it is generally possible loosely to date the various woodland clearance and regeneration episodes.

In previous centuries farming and settlements were greatly influenced by environmental factors. People were at the mercy of the weather, and did not have either the technology or the capital investment necessary to exploit the land as intensively as nowadays. The consistently low level of rural productivity is reflected in the wealth and population statistics available for pre-industrial Lancashire (Buckalzsch 1950; Scofield 1965). The county was one of the poorest and least densely populated in the whole country. In 1225 only Devon had a lower tax assessment; in 1334 Lancashire came second to Northumberland. In 1377 Lancashire's recorded population density was less than half that of parts of the Midlands and East Anglia. Even as late as 1707, Lancashire's assessment for tax was only around two-fifths that of Cheshire's.

River crossings

The focus of historic Lancashire was its county town, Lancaster. This became the administrative centre for Roger of Poitou's estates; he erected a fine castle there and endowed the priory (Pl. 10). Lancaster lies at the tidal limit and lowest bridging-point of the Lune, looking north-west across Morecambe Bay to the peninsulas of Furness and Cartmel, and south across to Cockerham, the mouth of the Wyre and the Fylde. From Lancaster there ran routes across the sands of Morecambe Bay to service Lancashire North of the Sands (as Furness and Cartmel became known), routes still in use today as tourist attractions. The shifting sands of the Leven and Kent estuaries at the top end of the bay make an experienced guide a necessity, and the proprietors of the Cumberland Pacquet in 1781 took care that they had 'procured a sober and careful driver, who is well acquainted with the sands' (Fell 1884). Conishead Priory was charged with the office of guide over Leven Sands, an office that survived the Dissolution and the coming of the railway. Various Charitable Trusts Acts secured the endowments of the guides over the Kent and Levens Sands into the twentieth century and the *Victoria County History* noted that in 1899 two persons a day, on average, were crossing the Kent Sands (VCH, VIII: 127).

There have been many fatalities over the years. Amongst the earliest recorded is the death of Michael, son of William le Fleming III, who died on 21 March 1268/69 when attempting to cross Leven Sands from Cartmel Priory to his manor at Aldingham. In 1325 the Abbot of Furness wrote of the 'great mortality of the people of Furness . . . passing and returning across the sands at the ebb of the tide who are often caught and drowned to the numbers of sixteen at a time'. The burial registers of Cartmel church list 141 casualties of the crossings between 1559 and 1880 and John 'Iron Mad' Wilkinson is said to have lost his life by 'the overwhelming in quicksand' of the coach in which he was travelling in the passage over Kent Sands in 1808. Not surprisingly, local residents like Sir Thomas Lowther of Holker in the 1720s took care to warn intending visitors not to risk crossing over both sets of sands in one tide, and 'to make the coach as little heavy in things as possible'. Although dangerous and usable only at low tide, these cross-sands routes give a considerably shorter travel time, avoiding overland routes along the sands and mosses flanking the rivers inland. The distance from Lancaster to Ulverston across the sands is only twenty miles, contrasted with thirty-four by the 'new road' of 1820. The short route was useful for both the casual traveller and marauding Scots! On more than one occasion in the fourteenth century surprise attacks were launched upon Lancashire South of the Sands.

The importance of the over-sands route emphasises the problems encountered by travellers on the overland routes. The mosses flanking the main river systems were a major barrier to north-south travel. As a consequence, river and coastal transport played an important role in the communications history of the county. Log-boats could move along the mainly east-west flowing rivers to the sea; passengers and cargo could then transfer to seagoing vessels and sail north or south along the Irish Sea coastline. In this way north-west Britain was united by the Irish Sea and it was possible to travel from Wales to Scotland via Lancashire, the Isle of Man or Ireland, as desired. On land, the river valley routes acted as major communication channels. Frequently Roman roads, and later roads, canals and railways, followed the valleys east-west across the Pennines (Fig. 1.3). It is often impossible to distinguish between roads and rivers as the main vehicle for access into an area – or egress from it. It is probably unfair even to attempt the exercise. River valleys were obviously important for settlement in the North-West, the coincidence of communication routes reinforcing the need to have an available supply of water. River terrace deposits commonly provided fertile land for cultivation as well as reasonably well-drained sites for habitations. Not surprisingly, early settlements were often sited close to rivers so as to exploit the advantages to the full.

Crossings on the major rivers tended to be concentrated along a limited stretch of the river because of the difficulty in finding suitable places to cross. Communication nodes developed at these crossing-points; sometimes several routes met there. The Manchester–Salford area is a good example. Roads from Chester, York, Ribchester, Wigan and Glossop met and crossed the Irwell at Manchester. Settlements were attracted to this communication node, hence the growth of Salford on one side of the Irwell, and Manchester on the other side. Another nodal point can be found at the tidal limit of the Ribble, around Preston, Penwortham and Walton-le-Dale. A third can be found on the Mersey, with Warrington on the north bank and Wilderspool and Thelwall on the south bank. It is important to recognise that there is rarely one single crossing-point; instead one finds a more or less loosely-

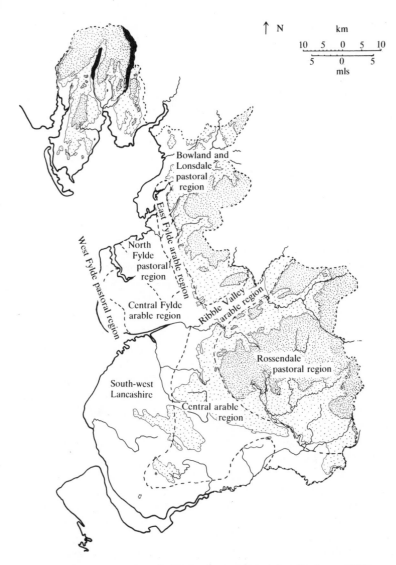

Fig. 1.3 Land-use regions in Tudor Lancashire (after Rodgers 1955)
Rodgers used the evidence of Final Concords to categorise the various
topographical regions

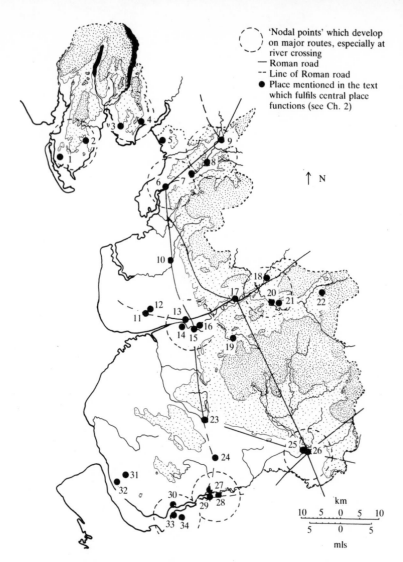

Fig. 1.4 Communication nodes in Lancashire

Key 1 – Furness, 2 – Skelmore Heads, 3 – Cartmel, 4 – Castle Head, 5 – Warton, 6 – Lancaster, 7 – Halton, 8 – Hornby, 9 – Burrow-in-Lonsdale, 10 – Garstang, 11 – Kirkham, 12 – Treales, 13 – Preston, 14 – Penwortham, 15 – Walton-le-Dale, 16 – Cuerdale, 17 – Ribchester, 18 – Clitheroe, 19 – Blackburn, 20 – Whalley, 21 – Portfield, 22 – Castercliffe, 23 – Wigan, 24 – Newton-in-Makerfield, 25 – Salford, 26 – Manchester, 27 – Warrington, 28 – Thelwall*, 29 – Wilderspool*, 30 – Widnes, 31 – West Derby, 32 – Liverpool, 33 – Runcorn*, 34 – Halton**places in the historic county of Cheshire defined stretch of river being used. Over time, the focus frequently moves along the river according to shifts in the course of the river and its channels. Sometimes other factors may be involved as well, for example considerations of defence. These will be considered in more detail in later chapters. The Roman road system introduced a degree of stability for these crossing-points, but equally important is the way the Roman network formalised the north-south route along the narrow corridor now occupied by the A6, M6 and the main railway line to Scotland along the landward edge of the Fylde Plain.

It has been shown how the Irish Sea can be regarded as a unifying factor, linking the Celtic populations of north-west Britain (Chadwick 1970). Communications with the rest of mainland Britain seem to have been mostly by overland routes: they were slow and difficult. This part of the North-West was still remote from the heartland of the country. At the end of the twentieth century it can take less than two and a half hours to reach Manchester from London by train. It was a journey taking several days, if not weeks, in the twelfth-century, and was clearly not to be undertaken lightly, especially in winter. Earlier, between the seventh and eleventh centuries, the area which became Lancashire was a distant south-western corner of the kingdom of Northumbria. The heartland of the kingdom lay far to the east, not an hour or so on the train but several days' journey across the bleak expanse of the Pennines. Not only was Lancashire then a relatively poor and unpopulous region, but it was also remote from the seats of power of the Anglo-Saxon and medieval English kingdoms.

Lancashire's remoteness from central authority posed administrative problems and it was only possible to maintain political control by delegation, with the help of loyal thegns and barons, with the support of the church and crown nominees. On more than one occasion control of this part of the North-West was vested in a member of the royal family. The honour of Lancaster became an earldom and ultimately a duchy and palatinate. Since 1399, after the accession of Henry Bolingbroke (also known as Henry of Lancaster), the duchy has been held by the reigning monarch. Lancashire's remoteness did not result in a lack of interest on the part of the government – often quite the reverse. From Roman times onwards, administrations frequently became involved in the North-West for military reasons. For the Romans,

B

the North-West was a staging post, for garrisons and supplies, for the conquest of northern Britain. In the tenth century it was a bulwark against the Scandinavians; in the fourteenth it was a bulwark against the Scots. Military considerations frequently outweighed agricultural considerations – hardly an incentive to agricultural investment.

Given Lancashire's relatively poor environment, the rain, cool weather, vast expanses of moor and moss, in some ways it is a wonder that the county survived as long as 800 years. Even more surprising, perhaps, is the spirit of fierce pride and independence displayed by those who are native to the 'Red Rose County'. The badge owes as much to Shakespeare's imagination as to fifteenth-century politics at the time of the so-called 'Wars of the Roses'. The first appearance of the red rose as the symbol for Lancaster is found in his play *Henry IV, Part I*. But even if the rose symbol is a relatively recent introduction, the traditional loyalty is not. Local partisanship and antipathy to national rule are a feature of much of the north of Britain and predate modern politics by centuries, if not millennia. The creation of the county palatine of Lancaster, with its independent administrative and judicial machinery, only reinforced Lancashire's feeling of separateness. Even after Henry of Lancaster won the crown, his patrimony, the Duchy of Lancaster, remained separate and distinct from crown lands, under the authority of its own officials.

Parish, township and shire

The medieval townships were thinly inhabited and frequently covered vast areas. Large townships are common in upland areas, for example, Anglezarke, Quernmore and Over Wyresdale. They are also encountered in lowland moss areas, as shown by Pilling, Lathom, Burscough and Worsley. Where small townships do occur, almost without exception they lie in the more densely-populated lowlands, along river valleys and especially in the Manchester embayment. Some of these townships owed their independent status to post-medieval developments, industrial and urban. Elsewhere, as in the Fylde for instance, an area heavily settled by the eleventh century, the relative settlement density has decreased. As a consequence joint townships like Weeton with

Preese, Ribby with Wrea and Clifton with Salwick are common there. These were nearly all separate Domesday vills.

It is not surprising that small ecclesiastical parishes are rare in Lancashire. Single-township parishes are exceptional. They do occur, however, as for example at Heysham, Radcliffe and Ashton-under-Lyne. Large multi-township parishes are the rule. The majority of Lancashire's fifty-six pre-Reformation parishes contained between two and ten townships, though Whalley was exceptional with as many as forty-five townships. Fellows-Jensen's comparison of the mean size of ecclesiastical parishes in the north-western counties (based on data collected in 1931) shows that Lancashire had the largest parishes in the whole region, with a mean of 40 sq mls compared with Cheshire's 16 sq mls, Cumberland's 17 sq mls and Westmorland's 25 sq mls (Fellows-Jensen, 1985: 386).

Township and parish boundaries were not absolutely fixed until post-Conquest times in many parts of the county. The less intensive pattern of exploitation of the landscape found in early Lancashire did not require firm boundary divisions. The practice of intercommoning, whereby two or more townships shared pastures, inhibited boundary formation in upland areas. Furness Fell was not partitioned until the twelfth century. Numerous mosses were subject to arguments concerning boundaries in late medieval and post-medieval times. Even today two intercommoning areas still remain in Lancashire North of the Sands. These are Birkrigg Common (Pl. 4), shared by Urswick and Aldingham, and Gawthwaite Moor in Ulverston Parish, common to Lowick and Lower Subberthwaite. Tithes, which became formally established during the later Anglo-Saxon period as a major source of church income, contributed to the definition of boundaries.

Lancashire's long-standing rural poverty helps to explain its relatively late development as a single territorial unit. Elsewhere in England there is a strong thread of territorial continuity from later prehistoric tribal kingdoms to medieval times. Firm links have been established connecting tribal centres and Romano-British population centres, as for instance the Cornovian centre at successively the Wrekin, and then *Virconium* (Wroxeter). Shrewsbury, further along the Severn, became the major regional focus during the medieval period. Another well-documented example is Cirencester, the medieval town on the site of Roman

Corinium, the *civitas Dobunnorum* which superseded the *oppidum* at nearby Bagendon. As will be shown in the following chapters, there are a few readily identifiable hillforts which could have acted as a population focus in Lancashire. None of these formed the basis for a Romano-British town. This contrasts with the situation to the east of the Pennines which formed the wealthier half of Brigantia. A Romano-British *civitas* capital (i.e. 'county town') was developed at *Isurium Brigantia* (Aldborough), which eclipsed the old tribal centre at Stanwick; the civilian settlement outside the fortress at York was awarded the status of a *colonia* in the third century. To the west of the Pennines, the needs of the native Brigantes for trade and exchange, for administrative centres, etc., were met by the civilian settlements (*vici*) and the forts on which they were dependent. Lancashire's development as a shire, on the other hand, is intimately bound up with the hundredal organisation of the tenth and eleventh centuries, and with territorial dispositions of the late eleventh century, in particular Roger of Poitou's holdings in north Lancashire. The welding together of these territorial units into a single shire, the knitting together of estates lying both North and South of the Sands, belongs to the twelfth century when the county first came into being.

The strong thread of continuity of exploitation of certain natural resources and communication nodes is one of the themes explored in the following chapters. The early history of the area which became the historic county of Lancaster will be traced, and special attention will be paid to the development and organisation of settlements within the landscape. The origins of the medieval lordships and baronies which coalesced to form the shire will be examined, and it will be shown how they arose out of earlier estate groupings and British lordships. These early estate groupings will in turn be related to postulated hillfort territories of the first millennium BC which developed to exploit and control the major natural communication routes from the Lake District to the Irish Sea coast, and across the Pennines to the Yorkshire Wolds.

2

The first millennium BC

Typically this part of the North-West merits a few sentences, perhaps the odd paragraph or two, in general books describing British prehistory. The reasons for this are easy to find as one looks around museum displays searching for exhibits from the period. With few exceptions there is a distinct lack of 'glamour' about the finds. All too often the displays consist of a case or so of flints, stone and metal axes, and potsherds carefully arranged to demonstrate technological progress. Even though this is slowly changing, nonetheless, archaeological awareness in the region is still heavily influenced by finds rather than sites: a museum display is undeniably more accessible than the average prehistoric site in the North-West and certainly more intelligible.

The lack of material objects surviving from the prehistoric period is mirrored by the poverty and paucity of the sites. The relatively poor environment in the North-West was an important determinant for the way that settlement and territorial organisation developed in the region. This is not to say that it was the only factor, or even necessarily the principal one. Yet poor soils, vulnerability to coastal changes and marginality for cereal production have all influenced the pattern of resource exploitation. The availability of natural resources did not remain static and unchanging over time and population levels varied considerably according to the carrying capacity of the land. As noted in the previous chapter, climatic variations did affect the lower and, more especially perhaps, the upper limits of cultivation and settlement. According to the currently available evidence the climate warmed up gradually, though unevenly, after the retreat of the main ice sheets. It was at its warmest during the earlier centuries of the Neolithic period, with average temperatures around three degrees higher than today's norm. Average rainfall was probably around 10 per cent higher than now. By the time of the Elm Decline (around 5,000 years ago) it had become cooler and drier, so that by the late Neolithic period temperatures and rainfall were roughly similar to today's. During the Bronze Age climatic conditions worsened, becoming appreciably cooler and wetter by around 1,000 BC. The wetter weather resulted in a renewed growth in many of the peat bogs in north-west Europe, and growth horizons have been noted in Danish bogs as well as in deposits in England. Lancashire examples are known from areas North and South of the Sands, from Rusland and Holcroft, as well as from sites on the periphery of the county like Wessenden near Oldham. Soil erosion (resulting from early prehistoric clearance activity) was a contributory factor for peat growth, especially in upland areas. The combination of anthropogenic and environmental factors combined to reduce the carrying capacity of upland regions like the Pennines which are largely uninhabited today. The trend of climatic deterioration was not reversed until well after around 500 BC, when it gradually gave way to the warmer and drier weather experienced under Roman rule. Vineyards were established in several parts of England – if not in the North-West – and it again became possible to exploit the uplands on a limited scale for agricultural and settlement purposes.

Early territories in the North-West

One of the major themes of this book is the absence of territorial unity in earlier times: there is no territorial – or social – cohesion to the area later known as Lancashire which can be shown, or even suggested, by reference to the archaeological record. Yet it is possible to catch glimpses of earlier patterns of territorial organisation underlying the ancient county. These are not necessarily territories which have any sort of political unity in the modern sense. They are territories based on the exploitation of natural resources as much as on the control of crossing-places and other strategic considerations.

Already by the Mesolithic period small communities of hunter–

gathers were exploiting sites in the North-West. Thousands of Mesolithic flints have been found along the central Pennine uplands in Lancashire. The communities exploiting these uplands – hunting red deer for example – on a seasonal basis will have had base camps lying at a lower altitude for use in the winter. This implies an extensive resource territory, though quite how extensive is open to question. Some time around 4,000–3,000 BC a change began to appear in the pattern of exploitation of the landscape. Communities which until then had been peripatetic within fairly fixed territories began to make clearances for agriculture and became more settled. This change is marked in the pollen record as the 'Elm Decline'. Elm pollen values are dramatically reduced in deposits of this date across the whole country, as a result of natural causes (e.g. disease) and/or because of selective felling by man. The best documented example in Lancashire is Red Moss near Horwich where the decline is quite early, around 5,060 ±80bp. As population levels increased and communities became more permanently settled there was more likelihood of conflict and social stress than in earlier times, when family-based communities were exploiting relatively empty environments. Responses included the development of social identities and the beginning of a definition of territories. Definition took various forms and the Neolithic and following metalworking period are characterised by megalithic momuments, tumuli and other earthworks. Three examples are known in Lancashire. Pikestones, 275 m up on Anglezarke Moor, is the remains of a chambered cairn; Calderstones near Liverpool is a passage grave with Irish affinities; and a long barrow lies on the northern slope of Skelmore Heads near Ulverston. Mention may also be made of the wood henge at Bleasdale, situated at the interface of the Fylde Plain and the Bowland foothills. There are far too few sites west of the Pennines to be able to offer much analysis of probable territories before the first millennium BC, but these ceremonial and ritual sites can be interpreted as territorial indicators, the symbolic markers of early social territories.

Territories in the first millenium BC

It is difficult to apply the conventional three-age system (stone, bronze, iron) in the North-West. Indeed, in many ways the first millennium BC in the North-West can be regarded as forming a cultural continuum. Despite the availability of new metalworking technologies, the appearance of 'new' forms of burial rites and of defensive earthworks during the first half of the millennium, the underlying population shows little evidence of change. The North-West remained a largely aceramic, impoverished, cultural backwater, far removed from the wealth and symbols of power which characterised first Wessex and then other parts of southern England which were in close contact with mainstream developments on the Continent. The opening of the millennium saw a significant worsening of the climate. The effect on the local population will have been to reduce productivity on marginal soils, putting better-drained land at a premium. The major period of hillfort building/refurbishment of defences seems to follow on from this deterioration of the climate and may in part reflect increased social tensions and territorial stress. None of the Lancashire hillforts has been thoroughly excavated: in most cases information is restricted to details concerning unstratified finds and sections through the defences. It is ironic that some of the best evidence derives from Portfield near Whalley. This site has suffered serious damage from trenching for water pipelines between 1953 and 1974. Further damage occurred when the ownership of Portfield Farm changed hands some twenty years ago. The new farmer was unaware of the hillfort's existence and unhappily levelled part of the northern defences (Beswick and Coombs 1986).

This absence of excavated material means that questions concerning the character and chronology of the sites cannot be answered. More importantly, one cannot determine which sites were contemporary. On the basis of analogies from elsewhere in the North it is highly unlikely that any of the defended hilltop sites were occupied after the fifth century BC – a significant point when one comes to consider the wider territorial implications of the distribution of hillforts in the north of England. In terms of the North-West, several points must be raised before proceeding to consider individual examples. Firstly, there is an apparent grouping of the hillforts. Even if allowance is made for the availability of suitable hilltop sites, the hillforts are not evenly scattered across the whole region. One grouping has been noted around the northern fringes of Morecambe Bay, from Millom in Cumbria

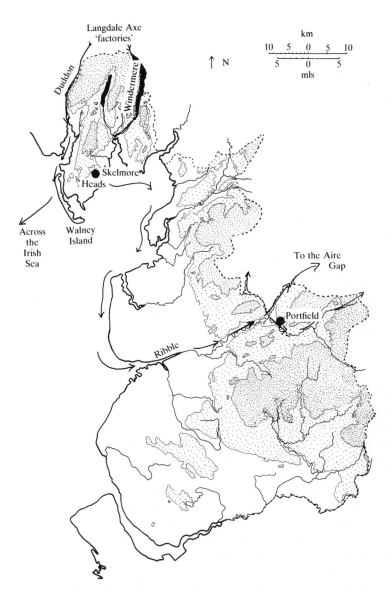

Fig. 2.2 Transmission routes for Cumbrian axes

to Walney (Fig. 2.2). Activity on the beach at Walney Island is represented from at least the fifth millennium BC, right through the Neolithic and metalworking periods. This activity included flintworking (using either local beach flints or even imported Irish material) and finishing of Cumbrian stone axes. Beaker pottery and Neolithic grooved ware have been found on the island. Another route ran along Lake Windermere, down the valley of the Leven towards Castle Head and the estuary. From the northern end of the Bay axes were then transmitted along the Irish Sea littoral and possibly thence from the Ribble estuary to the Ribble–Aire Gap and the Yorkshire Wolds (see below). Finds of Cumbrian axes in Ireland indicate contacts across the sea, a link confirmed by the close parallels between the large early stone circle at Swinside and that at Ballynoe in Ireland. Swinside, which lies on the west side of the Duddon (SD 172883), was probably the social focus for the whole of southern Lakeland in the Neolithic period and can be compared with Long Meg and her Daughters further north. Both have been linked with the Cumbrian axe trade (Waterhouse 1985; Higham 1986).

The importance of these routes into – and out of – the Lake District central massif continued through the metalworking period. The Ambleside hoard of bronzes (dated c. 1,200–1,000 BC) is a type hoard for the Penard phase of metalworking in Britain. It can be associated with the repeated use of this route along Lake Windermere and the Leven to Morecambe Bay. Across from Cartmel, the Low Furness communities continued to flourish. There are numerous cairns and small stone circles throughout the peninsula, including the concentric circles on Birkrigg Common known as Druids Circle. Several settlement sites are indicated on the Ordnance Survey map of the area, though one of the Stainton sites, Stone Close, has been lost to quarrying. There must be a strong presumption that some of these settlements had an early origin. Stone Close yielded finds of roughed-out and polished Cumbrian axes as well as a bronze palstave and a socketed axe. Several other socketed bronze axes are known from the vicinity, including six found just outside the southern boundary of the hillfort at Skelmore Heads. This last-mentioned hoard is especially interesting as it included one axe straight from the mould and two 'seconds'. Powell et al. (1963) suggest that this represents the stock of a smith, suggesting a parallel with the Portfield hoard (see below). Both were clearly high-status sites where the services of a smith were in demand.

Pottery is scarce from these sites. Besides the grooved ware and parts of a Beaker from Walney Island fragments of an urn have been reported from Great Urswick. Beaker fragments are known from Levens Park and from Dog Holes Cave at Warton. This scatter of Beakers is significant. It may suggest an east–west linkage across north Lancashire via the Lune and its tributaries to the Craven district of Yorkshire where there is a concentration of Beaker finds, or, less likely perhaps, a link via the coast route and the Ribble.

The full pattern of hillforts and postulated territories inland from the radial territories of Morecambe Bay has yet to be determined. Forde-Johnson (1962) has suggested that a later prehistoric hillfort underlies the motte-and-bailey castle at Hornby (SD 582698), which sits on a low promontory (35 m) overlooking the flood plain at the confluence of the Lune and Wenning to the south and the confluence of the Lune and Greta to the north (Pl. 5). Such a site would have obvious strategic advantages. It commands the crossing of the Lune and its tributaries there, used today by several roads including the main Lancaster to Skipton road (A687). The strategic advantage of Hornby was recognised in Norman times when Hornby was the seat of the Montbegon lordship. A strategic territory based here would also be well situated to exploit the fertile soils of the valley floors as well as upland pastures. A little further upriver Castle Hill, Leck (SD 651779, 200 m OD), which lies between the Leck Beck and the Greta, has been claimed as the site of another hillfort. This is a roughly circular enclosure of under one hectare surrounded by an internal ditch and external bank, and is really only a defended farmstead. Continuing along the Greta one arrives at the (undisputed) major hillfort of Ingleborough (SD 741746) which lies just across the border in Yorkshire. The hillfort sits on the top of Ingleborough Common, a limestone summit which attains 723 m. It crowns a limestone massif bordered by the headwaters of the Greta along the north, the headwaters of the Wenning to the south and the headwaters of the Ribble along its eastern edge. Technically outside Lancashire, Ingleborough was obviously sited to exploit the territory which straddled the Lancashire–Yorkshire–Westmorland borders. The hillfort is still marked by its stone

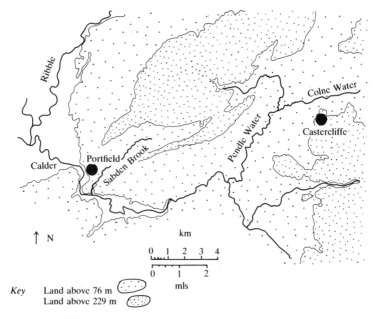

Fig. 2.3 Hillforts in the Whalley area

walling which encloses 6 ha and its defensive circuit is clearly of an early type. In 1855 nineteen hut circles could be discerned within its interior. The hillfort's strategic importance for the command of the routes traversing the headwaters of the rivers listed above is obvious.

The Portfield and Whalley area

Portfield (SD 746355, 121 m OD) lies in the interface zone between the western flanks of the central Pennines and the lowlands associated with the valley of the lower Ribble and its tributaries (Fig. 2.3). It is a small promontory hillfort sitting 90 m above the Calder, 4 km upstream from its confluence with the Ribble. In former times an area of approximately 1·4 ha was enclosed by two ramparts. As might be expected, the external defences were most marked on the northern side where the natural contours afforded least protection. On the northern side, before levelling in 1970, there was a 6 m-wide rampart, as well as an outer ditch and counterscarp bank which ran on a slightly different alignment. On the south there was another rampart, perhaps with an internal palisade. To the west the perimeter is defined by a steep natural scarp descending to the valley floor. Extensive trenching for the four water pipelines has destroyed much of the interior and excavators were unable to draw up a coherent plan of any structures from the post holes and other features picked up during the limited excavations (Beswick and Coombs 1986). Large-scale excavations ('area-stripping') would be necessary to elucidate the internal arrangements.

Nevertheless, despite the difficulties facing excavators, it is clear that activity on the site was not restricted to a single episode of defensive use. Pockets of activity were recorded across the site which have been dated from the Neolithic period onwards. The earliest datable material, represented by leaf arrowheads, pits and a chert-knapping floor, suggest fairly substantial Neolithic occupation. The Neolithic finds are widely distributed across the site and, though there is no evidence to associate this activity with any defensive structure, the excavators did not rule out the possibility. The high status of Portfield in the third millennium BC is indicated by finds of Grimston-style pottery. Neolithic pottery is generally rare to the west of the Pennines. More is being recovered by archaeologists, such as the Mortlake bowl found during excavations at the *vicus* of the Roman fort at Lancaster, but it is unlikely that future discoveries will reduce the significance of the Portfield material.

Portfield's importance in this period stems from its position on the distribution network for Cumbrian stone axes. Find spots (?trading losses) are known in the vicinity, from Pendle, Wiswell and Upbrook Farm near Clitheroe. There was obviously a close relationship with the richer, agricultural-based communities to the east of the Pennines, especially those in the Yorkshire and Lincolnshire Wolds where finds of Cumbrian axes are predominant. This link with the Wolds was effected along one of the central Pennine communication corridors, most likely via the Ribble–Aire Gap, though a route from the Calder to the Colne–Keighley Pass is feasible. It is worth recalling the thousands of worked flints of the Mesolithic period: those found on the moors above Burnley at Briercliffe, Worsthorne and Trawden; and those from further south on the Anglezarke–Rivington Moors and from the Heywood–Rochdale–Saddleworth area. Quantities of 'imported' flints have been identified at some of these upland sites, suggesting an early link with south-east Yorkshire and north Lincolnshire. Once established, these communication corridors across the Pennines continued to flourish. The Aire Gap was also used as a channel for the transmission of Irish influences and material. The hoard of three flat axes from Read near Whalley, for example, contained one Irish type.

There was possibly a break in the activity at Portfield during the early metalworking period. Nothing diagnostically early Bronze Age has been recognised despite the numerous burial and ritual monuments in the area. These include the major complex of fourteen small stone circles, tumuli, and other features within 24 sq km on the moors around Burnley. The main period of defences at Portfield belong to the late Bronze Age, the years around 750–500 BC. The sequence is not entirely clear but there seem to have been at least two major phases of rampart building. The late Bronze Age hoard found by workmen digging in the fort interior in 1966 has been assigned a seventh-century BC date by scholars at the British Museum (Longworth 1967) and it is therefore likely to be contemporary with the main defences. Beside two bronze axes and five other bronze items, two gold objects were found, a penannular tress-ring and a bracelet. The hoard is generally considered to represent the property of a bronze smith because of its scrap metal component. The cultural affinities of the metalwork lie with the contemporary north British and Irish industries. Similar features are found in another late Bronze Age hoard from Lancashire, that from Winmarleigh on the mossland edge just north of Garstang. Both hoards included a baggy faceted axe (Gillespie type) of a type that occurs in a north-western British distribution from South Argyllshire to Lancashire. Significantly, a third axe of this type has been found at Stainton Quarry near Skelmore Heads.

Castercliffe (SD 884388, above 360 m OD), a small oval contour fort lying 14·4 km to the west, must be broadly contemporary with the main phase of occupation of Portfield hillfort. Originally three ramparts enclosed the 1·7 ha site. Disappointingly, there have been no finds other than unstratified flints over the years. Radiocarbon dates for the ramparts of around 510 ±70bp confirm that the likely occupation occurred between 750 and 500 BC (Coombs

1982). Castercliffe immediately overlooks the valley of Pendle Water. This valley was chosen for the Leeds–Liverpool Canal and is another natural routeway across to the Aire Gap. Its use in Roman and Medieval times is exemplified by the fort at Elslack, the villa at Gargrave, and by Skipton Castle.

The relationship between the two hillforts is puzzling. Did they share the same resource territory? Do they represent two contemporary or consecutive strategic territories on the Ribble–Aire route? It may be significant that Castercliffe is of an entirely different type from the other Lancashire hillforts, being a contour rather than a promontory type. Its ramparts appear to be of different construction too, since they are apparently stone and timber laced. The inner rampart shows signs of vitrification. It may be that Castercliffe fits in better with the tradition represented by Eddisbury, Almondbury, etc., and that it occupied a higher place in the hierarchy, albeit one that was short lived. The absence of finds is even more striking. As noted above, the moors around Castercliffe and Portfield are rich in remains from the metalworking period. The Beaker burial from Extwistle Moor is not to be viewed in isolation but as an indication of a continuing tradition of high-status activity in the locality. The radiocarbon date for the earliest clearance of the woodland at one site on Extwistle Moor, 310 ±100bc, is proof that the area continued to be exploited even after the hillforts had been abandoned.

So far only a handful of defended hilltop sites have been investigated in Lancashire. Typically they are small promontory-style forts, closer in appearance to the forts in Cheshire (except Eddisbury) than to the large multivallate contour forts of the central Pennines exemplified by Mam Tor and Almondbury. Besides the ones already discussed, Forde-Johnson (1962) has conducted a trial excavation of the defences of a site named Camp Hill in the Liverpool area (SD 424858) and Hallam (1986) has suggested that there is a potential hillfort at Hawsclough (and a more dubious second at Dovecote) in Clayton-le-Woods. What appears to be a small univallate promontory site has recently been excavated at Walmersley near Bury (SD 797130, Fletcher 1986). This last site begins to fill in a major gap in the distribution of later prehistoric sites around the Manchester embayment. Rossendale Forest has produced numerous finds of flints from the Mesolithic period, and various weapons and implements from the Neolithic and metalworking period. Several Bronze Age tumuli are known. It is inherently unlikely that the area failed to function as some sort of territorial 'unit' during the later prehistoric period and the site at Walmersley offers a confirmation of the area's persistent status. It is probable that further small defended hilltop sites may be discovered in the future.

As the distribution stands, the hillforts in Lancashire can be seen to be located in areas where there was an established ritual/ ceremonial tradition, perhaps reflecting power bases which developed in association with the exchange network for Cumbrian axes. The precise mechanisms for the distribution (and redistribution) of high-status goods like axes are ill-understood. Anthropological parallels suggest several possibilities besides straightforward trading contacts. These include gift exchange and tribute relationships. Whatever the mechanism, the monopolistic manipulation of exchange procedures for high-status goods seems to have been as important as environmental factors for the success of resource territories in the prehistoric period. Control over communication nodes was a vital factor for the siting of hillforts and the definition of strategic territories on the local scale. Questions concerning the precise implications for the people living within these territories – whether they owed allegiance, tribute, labour, etc., to any specific hillfort, or indeed to a hierarchy of hillforts – must be left unanswered for the present.

Brigantia

Our ideas about the extent of tribal territories in the pre-Roman era are dominated by classical authors writing after the establishment of the Roman Empire. This is particularly true in the case of the Brigantes, about whom surprisingly little is known, especially when one considers the extent of Brigantia, and the fact that the first-century historian, Tacitus, considered them to be the most populous of all the native tribes in Britain (Hartley and Fitts 1988). In Roman times the northern limit of the tribal territory is thought to have extended into modern Dumfriesshire, where a third-century dedication to the tutelary goddess, Brigantia, had been found. Ptolemy, the second-century geographer, who listed various settlements within their territory, recorded that their lands stretched from sea to sea. According to him their southern border marched with those of the Cornovii in the west and the Corieltauvi to the east of the Pennines. Chester certainly lay within Cornovia and many people take the Mersey as marking the southern limit of Brigantia.

But one must beware of regarding rivers as an finite linear boundary in this period. For although this is certainly the case below Warrington, the boundary may have been more flexible further upriver. Given the extent of the mosses flanking the middle reaches of the Mersey, it may be preferable to see the Mersey mossland belt between Warrington and Manchester as a frontier zone between the two tribal territories and not to treat all the land lying to the south of the river as automatically belonging to the Cornovii. One cannot rule out the possibility of a tribal subdivision straddling the mosses and extending into what became north-east Cheshire. Shallow-drafted log-boats could have provided a means of communication along and across the river, as in later times. The remains of Lindow Man and at least one other bog body were recovered from a moss on the edge of Wilmslow (Cheshire) in the 1980s (Stead *et al.* 1986). They have been assigned radiocarbon dates which would fall within the early Roman period. This has prompted Ross's hypothesis that they might have been sacrifices made in a last-ditch attempt to ward off the Roman invasion of the North-West (Ross 1989). Setting aside this contentious theory, it is pertinent to ask whether the sacred pool in the moss lay on the Brigantian or the Cornovian side of the border zone. It is a question that is unlikely ever to be answered. Another broadly contemporary bog body is known from Worsley, north of the Mersey. This may or may not be significant. It should be remembered that sacrifices in bogs are part of a wider north-west European cultural tradition, the most famous examples of which derive from Denmark and north Germany.

The Brigantes were not, of course, a single tribe, but a grouping of a number of small tribal units sometimes called clans or septs. The names of several of these smaller tribes are known. Some, like the Tectoverdi and Lopocares, were based to the east of the Pennines; others, like the Carvetii (Higham and Jones 1985) and Setantii, can be located to the west of the Pennines. The Carvetii seem to have been based in the Eden valley, and later became an individually identifiable tribal unit presumably focused on Carlisle. The Setantii were located to their south. Ptolemy writes of the

Portus Setantiorum, which is commonly accepted to have been a lost Romano-British port at the mouth of the Wyre. It is not known whether the Setantii extended beyond the Fylde Plain into the remainder of what became Lancashire, or even whether they fell within the wider territory controlled from Portfield in the middle of the first millennium BC. Evidence for later prehistoric activity in and around the Fylde is not lacking. Numerous Bronze Age burials are known, and there have been many stray finds of metalwork spanning the period. The best known is the Winmarleigh hoard of late bronzes (*c.* 850–*c.* 500 BC), found just to the north of Garstang. Its affinities with the Portfield hoard have already been mentioned. Mention must also be made of the Pilling Sword, found on Coptham Farm during ploughing in 1917 and since lost, and of the later bronze scabbard decorated in the La Tène style recovered from Pilling Moss. Swords are rare in the North-West and the presence of these finds gives an indication of the relative status of the area at the close of the first millennium.

The origin of these smaller tribes which came to make up the Brigantes is lost in prehistory. They had no doubt developed more or less locally according to the geography, economy and social organisation of a region. They must somehow be linked with the territories which grew up during the first part of the first millennium BC, though there is a considerable gap between the last-known occupation of the hillforts around the fifth century BC and the appearance of these tribes in the historical record. Attempts have been made, however, to link the hillforts with Ptolemy's Brigantian centres. Ingleborough, for example, has been equated with *Rigodunum*, but this attribution has been disputed. The Roman fort at Castleshaw has been put forward as an alternative.

It seems that after the tensions of the second quarter of the first millennium BC, which saw the construction of defensive hilltop sites, the North was sufficiently free from external and internal tensions and pressures to render the hillforts redundant, unless, of course, our interpretation of the situation is completely wrong and there is a whole new class of defensive sites awaiting recognition. Why and how this should be the case is another unresolved puzzle. Higham (1987), contrasting the absence of activity in the hillforts in northern England with refurbishment and building further north, beyond the Tyne and Annan, has theorised that northern England had come under the sway of wealthier and more powerful communities living in the Yorkshire Wolds, who are later known as the Parisi. He notes that the abandonment of hillforts in the north is 'broadly contemporary' with the emergence of the Arras culture in east Yorkshire, and goes on to suggest that the east Yorkshire people established a hegemony throughout northern England, from the North Sea to the Irish Sea. This control was partly managed through a monopoly of luxury goods and burial customs, supported by their command of exchange mechanisms whereby slaves and raw materials were exported to Gaul and the Rhineland in return for imported luxuries. The name Parisi is also a continental import. If this is indeed the case, and it is an attractive theory, then it goes some way to explaining the situation. As shown earlier, the exchange route from the North-West to the Wolds has a long history going back to at least the third millennium and the 'export' of Cumbrian axes.

Culturally, at least, many of these subject peoples, especially those to the west of the Pennines, were still a Bronze Age people. The Parisi would have obtained the slaves and other commodities as tribute exacted from a native population of farmers and pastoralists, using this 'surplus' to sustain their conspicuous consumption. Some of the wealth would have been redistributed to local leaders, thereby putting them under a gift obligation to ensure their loyalty.

By the end of the first millennium, however, there had been an economic and demographic change. The Parisi seem to have lost their dominance over northern England and the core of the future Brigantian territory shifted to the eastern flanks of the Pennines. Climatic conditions had steadily begun to improve and it was once again feasible to exploit the upper valleys and foothills on both sides of the Pennines. The economic basis of such upland sites is not immediately obvious, however, especially to the visitor at the turn of the second millennium AD who is engulfed by a sense of isolation in the landscape of barren limestone crags around Ribblehead. But one must be wary of projecting our own observations too far back into the past. Prince's (1976) study of the altitudinal effect of climate on barley yields compared crops sown on the same day (13 April) at Cambridge, Lancaster and Malham (370+ m), which lies a little to the south of Ingleborough. Not surprisingly, the Cambridge crop reached maximum grain weight soonest, but the Malham crop still managed to ripen.

These trial crops were sown and reared using fertilisers and all the benefits available to agricultural researchers in order to ensure comparable soil conditions. There is good reason to think that relative yields could have been very different in prehistoric times as the upland soils would have been significantly poorer than lowland ones. What is indicated by the trials, however, is that the altitude in this part of the Pennines would not have prevented grain cultivation beyond the level of mere subsistence farming during the warmer climatic periods.

Unfortunately it is proving remarkably difficult to pinpoint sites unequivocally occupied in the two hundred years or so before the Roman conquest. The farmstead sites and field systems in the Ingleborough area between the Greta and the Ribble are well known, as are those around Skelmore Heads in Furness. These sites, which typically appear as small enclosed hut circles and adjacent field systems, are notoriously difficult to date. Hartley and Fitts (1988) prefer an Iron Age context for the hut circles around Ribblehead but where diagnostic material occurs, it tends, on the whole, to be Romano-British in date. This was the case at Eller Beck, just across the Lancashire border, where partial excavations of one farmstead yielded a small quantity of Romano-British pottery (Lowndes 1963). Further west, in Furness, the settlement complex known as Urswick Stone Walls was excavated in 1906 (Dobson 1907). Several large fragments of quernstones were found, plus a flint scraper, but no datable pottery. The excavators proposed an occupation date in the first or second centuries BC. They may have unduly favoured this period because it would give a good fit with the current (*c.* 1906) theory of hillfort chronology – since extended by almost a thousand years. The small engraved bronze strip which they used to reinforce their choice of date could as easily belong to the Romano-British period as to the earlier centuries.

A similar situation obtains in other lowland areas to the west of the Pennines. Several potential native sites have been identified along the Lune valley and along the edges of the Lancashire mosses. More are being discovered as a result of aerial surveys by Professor Barri Jones, Nick Higham, Rob Philpott, Adrian Olivier, and others based at the universities of Manchester and Lancaster. Romano-British pottery has been recovered from the native farmstead site at Little Woolden on the edge of Chat Moss near Salford, for example, though worked flints of a much earlier period have also been found there.

In all of these cases the first activity on the site predates the Roman occupation and it may be that the Roman period farmsteads are descendants of earlier, pre-Roman settlements. Work by Higham and Jones on native-style farmsteads in Cumbria suggests a parallel picture (Higham and Jones 1975; 1983). Whenever native sites are discovered the datable finds, usually pottery, are Roman, but there is a strong suspicion that the basics of agricultural practice, and probably also of settlement, remained the same from the later prehistoric period until at least the second century AD.

This view is confirmed by the pollen diagrams covering the region (Fig. 2.4). Deforestation tends to be later to the west of the Pennines (especially in the southern Lakeland area) than to the east, where it is definitely associated with pre-Roman farming. Even so there is every reason to believe that the major woodland clearance phase began well before the advent of the Romans. The most representative pollen diagrams, those which give a regional rather than a purely localised picture, come from deposits of at least 100 m across. There is a reasonably good coverage for the region for the later prehistoric and Roman periods. One major drawback, however, is the rather inadequate dating of many of the samples. There are few radiocarbon-dated samples other than those from Rusland Moss (Furness). In several instances approximate dates are extrapolated on the basis of the rate of peat growth from one or two known dates, as is the case with the central Rossendale deposits. Elsewhere the presence of recurrence surfaces dated to the wetter and cooler periods around 500 BC and AD 500 allow a relative date to be assigned to many samples. Across most of the county, indeed across most of the country, the later prehistoric period saw the beginning of a major woodland clearance phase. This followed on after the pattern of sporadic, apparently short-lived clearances which characterised the early metalworking period in Lancashire. Trees were being cleared to make way for a more intensive exploitation of the landscape. These clearances were not solely for pastoral purposes, although Lancashire is traditionally regarded as having had a predominantly pastoral pattern of land-use in prehistoric times. There is evidence for the cultivation of cereals from places like Holcroft and Chat

Fig. 2.4 Location of pollen diagrams in the North-West

Key Pollen diagrams specifically mentioned in the text: 1 – Rusland,
2 – Pilling and Cockerham, 3 – Anglezarke and Rivington, 4 – Wessenden
near Oldham, 5 – Holcroft

Moss along the Mersey, and from deposits in the Rossendale uplands. As seen above, an increasing number of farmstead sites are being discovered in both upland and lowland areas.

It is against this background of a more widely-based agricultural economy that Brigantian hegemony emerged. Earlier authorities, like Piggot (1958), Richmond (1958) and Wheeler (1954), thought that the sole basis of the wealth of the Brigantes was vested in pastoralism which may even have involved a nomadic element. More recently it has been argued that pastoralism is an insufficient explanation and that there was more than mere subsistence agriculture. The discovery of so many native farmsteads loosely dated to the later prehistoric/Romano-British era supports this new view. These were permanent settlements occupied by people engaged in arable agriculture. On the other hand, one should not be too ready to dismiss the importance of cattle-raising, nor the wealth that it can provide. It can be argued that even in areas favourable for cereal cultivation livestock may be preferred as a more 'portable' form of wealth. This would be especially appropriate in areas where the level of lawlessness was high: cereal crops make vulnerable targets and constitute a large investment of labour. Cattle-rearing economies would also be more suited to a system of tribal organisation based on tribute renders that the Brigantes seem to have possessed.

The name Brigantes literally means 'the high ones'. Opinion is divided about whether this description should be interpreted literally or figuratively. Were the Brigantes originally 'the dwellers in the high place', i.e. the Pennines (the place name comes from British *penno- which means 'top, height, a hill' and, used adjectively, 'chief')? Or were they the 'high ones', 'the chief ones'? One suspects that the name originally began as a descriptive geographical term, but as the Brigantes established their hegemony over other northern tribes, the figurative term became more appropriate. The association may have been deliberately encouraged as a form of propaganda.

The pre-eminence of the Brigantes over the other northern tribes does not seem to have been long established when the Romans arrived, and one question that remains to be answered is when did this shift in the balance of political and economic power take place? Whether or not one accepts Higham's theory that the predecessors of the Parisi had exerted a supremacy over the small northern tribal communities, the establishment of the Brigantian hegemony, the welding together of the small tribes into a large unit under a single ruler, was clearly a later development. All the signs are that it happened in the first century AD rather than the first century BC. Several authorities are now proposing that the realignment took place in response to the threat from Rome (Hanson and Campbell 1986; Turnbull and Fitts 1988).

The end of Brigantia

Initially the Brigantes under Cartimandua seem to have been accorded client status by the Romans when they began their invasion and occupation of lowland Britain. By this time their major tribal centre was undoubtedly Stanwick, whose location between the Swale and the Tees on the eastern flanks of the Pennines reflects the geographical shift in their power structure. The nature of the site at Stanwick is only now being fully revealed. It is a massive centre whose enclosures extended over 300 ha at one point. It was occupied by the 40s AD, if not earlier, when considerable quantities of Roman pottery were arriving at the site. The presence of Roman tiles indicates Romanised building and it has even been suggested that Roman engineers were present to direct building operations on behalf of the client ruler. It is now becoming clear that Stanwick is a northern example of the enclosed *oppidum*, closer in conception to the tribal centres of southern Britain, Bagendon (Gloucestershire) and *Camulodunum* (Essex), than to hillforts like Portfield and Ingleborough (Turnbull 1984).

Exactly how long the Brigantes had been welded together as a single tribal unit is uncertain. Turnbull and Fitts (*BAR* 158) have suggested that Cartimandua, who first appears in the historical record in AD 51 when she surrendered Caractacus to the Romans, was the first and last paramount ruler of Brigantia. Others prefer to see her as a second-generation ruler, succeeding after the failure of the male line. Tacitus tells us that she was *pollens nobilitate* 'of noble lineage'. Female rulers are not unknown in first-century Britain and seem to have ruled whenever the male line died out. This is best exemplified by Boudicca's rule over the Iceni after her husband's death. Cartimandua, presumably for political and military reasons as much as for other considerations, had taken

Venutius as her consort. This relationship was not destined to last. There was fierce resentment amongst the northern communities directed against Cartimandua and her pro-Roman policies. Disaffection focused on Venutius, who emerged as the leader of the anti-Roman faction. Successive Roman governors were forced to send in their armies in attempts to bolster up Cartimandua's power during the 50s and 60s. This had the effect of partitioning lowland Yorkshire, denying the anti-Roman faction access to the lowland resource base.

Interpretations of troop dispositions have been bedevilled by efforts to reconcile the distribution of Roman camps and forts with Wheeler's interpretation of the respective bases of Venutius and Cartimandua. Wheeler, who excavated Stanwick between 1951 and 1952, believed that this was Venutius's base (Wheeler 1954). He located Cartimandua much further south, at Castle Hill, Almondbury (near Huddersfield). It is now accepted that Almondbury had long gone out of use by then and recent excavations at Stanwick (Turnbull 1984) have refuted its attribution to Venutius. Opinion currently favours Stanwick as the tribal capital of the pro-Roman client ruler, Cartimandua.

In AD 69, by which time Cartimandua had finally broken with Venutius, matters came to a head. Cartimandua had to be rescued by Roman troops, leaving Venutius in control of Brigantia. This led to a change in policy towards the North. The kingdom of Brigantia was no longer respected as a client but was invaded and then heavily garrisoned by the Roman army. The disposition of Roman troops on either side of the Pennines demonstrates the importance of the trans-Pennine communication corridors for the garrisoning of Brigantia as the whole of the north became one large strategic territory under Roman military authority. The natural east-west corridors through Lancashire formed the basis of the Chester–York route via Manchester, Castleshaw and Slack. Both it and the Ribble–Aire Gap (Fig. 1.4) via Kirkham, Ribchester, Elslack and Ilkeley were garrisoned by the end of the 70s at the latest. Roads were constructed along the line of these natural corridors, so linking the forts together and making permanent linear routes out of what had been more loosely-defined communication channels.

The temporary camps across Stainmore Pass may belong to this period. A pre-Flavian presence at Carlisle is indicated by finds of early pottery and coins. Pre-Flavian beginnings have also been suggested for Walton-le-Dale and Ribchester. This lends weight to the theory that Venutius was receiving support from west of the Pennines, if not operating from a base there in the 70s. Certainly by the time Agricola took up the post of governor of the province in 78 the North-West was used to the presence of Roman soldiers. Traditionally, however, it is Agricola who has been given credit for the establishment of Roman forts in the North-West. This is partly because his exploits are so well publicised, thanks to the writings of his son-in-law, Tacitus. He tells us that Agricola first secured his western flank, campaigning in Anglesey and North Wales, before directing his efforts to the north, consolidating and building upon the work of his predecessors. Agricola then moved up into Scotland. This rapid success was surely facilitated by the foundations laid down by Cerealis and Frontinus during the earlier part of the 70s.

On the basis of the available archaeological evidence, it seems likely that the forts of Manchester, Castleshaw (I) and Lancaster were built on Agricola's instructions, as was the new fort at Ribchester. These forts were all linked by the road network (Fig. 2.5). Manchester's location was especially significant. Not only did it lie on the major route connecting the two legionary for-tresses of York and Chester, but the north-south route through Ribchester on to Burrow and the Lune valley crossed here, as did several (later) lesser roads. These roads reinforced the nodal position of Manchester which was of great strategic importance for the control of the western part of Brigantia.

Agricola may have been responsible for the fort at Kirkham. This last site has not been fully excavated and relatively little is known about its chronology and layout. Shotter (1984) argues that it fits in with an offensive from the Ribble estuary inland, via Ribchester towards the Aire Gap. He also postulates a Roman military site in the Whalley area. The recognition of a Roman signal station on Mellor Hill illustrates the potential of the Ribble–Aire corridor for signalling purposes. As shown earlier in the chapter, the Ribble has a long history of use as a communication corridor and two hillforts were located in strategic positions over-looking tributaries of the Ribble in Lancashire. A small quantity of Roman pottery and an intaglio has been identified at one of these, Portfield. The excavator argued for some form of Roman

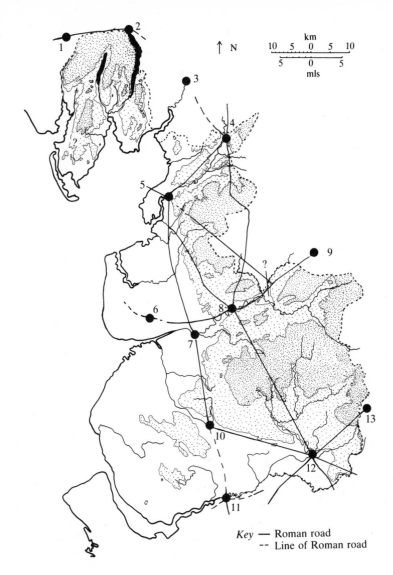

Fig. 2.5 Major Roman sites in the North-West

Notice the nodal position of Manchester. The fort lies at the intersection of north-south routes with the main east-west route linking the legionary fortresses of York and Chester

Key 1 – Hardknott, 2 – Ambleside, 3 – Watercrook, 4 – Burrow-in-Lonsdale, 5 – Lancaster, 6 – Kirkham, 7 – Walton-le-Dale, 8 – Ribchester, 9 – Elslack, 10 – Wigan, 11 – Wilderspool, 12 – Manchester, 13 – Castleshaw, ? – putative Roman site non-military activity of an obscure nature (Beswick and Coombs 1986).

The pattern of small forts (under 1·5 ha) like Castleshaw (I) and Slack, on the hills, and larger 2–2·5 ha forts like Ribchester and Manchester on the lowland fringes, testifies to the intensive military control of the western Pennines. These forts effectively policed the area, a visible and intimidating presence. Disaffection, if not absolute population levels, ran high in the North-West.

Agricola seems to have left the Lake District untouched. Under his successors a chain of forts was constructed in southern Lakeland, on Lancashire's northernmost border, from Watercrook near Kendal, to Ambleside at the top of Lake Windermere, across to Hardknott and finally reaching the coast at Ravenglass. The road linking these forts, Iter X of the Antonine Itinerary, is a spectacular piece of military engineering, especially where it crossed Hardknott Pass. The fort here, one of the best preserved in the north, is mentioned by Wordsworth in one of his sonnets. Although technically outside Lancashire, their proximity is such that the fells and lower-lying land further to the south must have fallen within their remit. The location of these forts continues the tradition of strategic policing of communication routes already familiar from Agricola's governorship. Ambleside, for example, controls the route followed by the Langdale axes down Lake Windermere. These forts therefore control entry to, and egress from the southern Lakeland lowlands. It is inconceivable that the relatively fertile and populous lowland area of Plain Furness was not itself garrisoned. There is a strong suspicion that a unit must have operated out of the Dalton area in the south-west corner of the Furness peninsula.

Not all of the forts were garrisoned throughout the Roman period. A number of garrisons in northern England were reduced, or removed altogether, during the middle decades of the second century. There is a conspicuous absence of a garrison along the York to Manchester road and the southernmost garrisoned trans-Pennine route was the Ribble–Aire Gap. Lancaster and some of the southern Lakeland forts were also decommissioned. The context for this is disputed. The need to man the new military installations required for the advance into Scotland may have been a major factor. On the other hand, one cannot ignore the local situation. The formerly extensive territory of the Brigantes had now been broken up, making a heavy 'police' presence redundant. Henceforth Brigantia was restricted to the territory around the *civitas* capital at Aldborough (*Isurium*) near Bainbridge. Some authors (Higham 1987, etc.) see this reduction in the territory as a punitive measure following upon opportunistic rebellion. This interpretation is based on the comments of Pausanius in his *Description of Greece* (8.43.3); he recorded that under Antoninus Pius the Brigantes were deprived of most of their territory on account of a war of aggression against the Genounii. This tribe has not been identified but the attack clearly would have presented the excuse, if one were needed, to break the Brigantian hegemony once and for all.

Tribal septs to the north and west were thereby freed of all allegiance to the Brigantes and were accorded a measure of independence. By the third century the Carvetii of the Eden valley had their own *civitas* capital, presumably at Carlisle (first attested 268). The Setantii in Lancashire would also have acquired their independence from what one may call 'Greater Brigantia'. Despite these measures, Brigantian unrest seems to have continued into the opening years of the third century and may have influenced Severus's decision to divide Britain into two provinces, Britannia Superior in the south, and a northern one, Britannia Inferior, based at York, of which Lancashire formed the south-western quarter.

The creation of the Roman province of Britannia Inferior testifies to one of the problems of ruling the North. As later Anglo-Saxon and medieval kings were to find, the North could not easily be ruled from a southern power base. Local feelings, whether of partisanship or perversity, run high, especially in the face of attempts by southern-based authorities to impose their laws, taxes and customs. Even within the North, internal rivalries are not to be disregarded and any would-be paramount ruler will have encountered problems when trying to weld together a hegemony made up of what was essentially little more than a loose grouping of tribes with different inherited traditions and practices. Several distinct strategic territorial units based on hillforts were identified in the area which became Lancashire. It is more than coincidence that post-Conquest parishes and lordships frequently mirrored these early territories. This is particularly noticeable in the north of the county where the fitz Reinfrid holding of Warton was established within the postulated territory of the hillfort at Warton Crags. The Montbegon lordship of Hornby has been linked with a potential hillfort underlying the motte- and-bailey castle. Medieval lordships also developed in Furness and Cartmel. Further south, the great de Lacy honour based on Clitheroe is surely located to exploit the same strategic territory as the hillforts of Castercliffe and Portfield. A strategic territory, however, is not the same as a natural resource territory and the two functions need to be carefully distinguished. Sometimes the two will be virtually conterminous, especially in geographically restricted areas like Furness. Elsewhere, although there will be overlap, the two may be quite separate. It will be argued in later chapters that the strategic territories focused on certain communication nodes were dictated by a range of considerations, some of them political, some defensive. Control of river crossings, for example, could move from one stretch or side of the river to another. Natural resource territories might exist on both sides, but only one would be the dominant strategic territory at any specific time. Similarly, the focus or 'control centre' of a natural resource territory would not necessarily be located in the same place as that of a strategic territory.

No one is claiming an unbroken tradition of lordship over 2,000 and more years, from the first millennium BC to the twelfth century AD, but there is demonstrable continuity in the patterns of exploitation of territorial units, especially the re-use of strategic territorial units, which made up the historic county.

3

The Romans in the North-West

Opening up the landscape

In the previous chapter the break-up of 'Greater Brigantia' was discussed. It fragmented into smaller tribal groupings like that of the Setantii during the course of the second century. The Setantii cannot be linked with any obvious first millennium BC hillfort territory and there is no evidence for any tribal centre associated with them. In fact, the only settlement nucleus which certainly lay within their territory was that associated with the fort at Kirkham. There appears to have been a substantial *vicus* but there are no indications that it survived the abandonment of the fort in the second century. In fact, with the exception of the *civitas* capital of the Carvetii, there are no Romano-British towns as such in the North-West. The garrison in Lancashire had been reduced but, unlike other parts of the country, there is no evidence for Romanisation in the form of recognisable urban settlements or villa estates. The nearest known villas are Gargrave in West Yorkshire and Eaton-by-Tarporley in Delamere Forest, Cheshire. In the South and Midlands, villas and towns acted as collecting points for fiscal impositions, and were an integral part of the redistribution network as agricultural produce was exchanged for consumer goods and luxury items. Why then were there no villas in Lancashire? The agricultural potential was certainly there during the Roman period. For, although it was a time of rising sea-levels which will have affected drainage along the coastal mosses, the

c

weather was much warmer and drier, improving conditions for cereal production. Arable cultivation spread up into the higher altitudinal margins for cultivation, as exemplified by native farmsteads at the headwaters of the Lune and Ribble and their tributaries. Settlements and field systems along the Leck Beck in north Lancashire lie at around the 300 m contour, which is well above today's limit for commercial cultivation.

On analogy with Cumbria, one would expect typical native farmsteads in Lancashire to be small sites, under a third of a hectare, composed of a circular or rectangular bank or ditch enclosing one or more circular huts. This appears to be the situation at the known but unexcavated site at Curlew Farm in the Fylde. The settlement at Curlew Farm, which has produced late first- to early second-century pottery, is a roughly univallate enclosure on the edge of what is now Rawcliffe Moss. The farmstead will have been able to exploit the alluvial deposits along the Wyre. An apparently similar farmstead has been located at Ryecroft Farm in the Rufford area, on the edge of Downholland Moss. Another single-ditched enclosure has recently been identified at Winwick.

Corroborative evidence for this opening-up of the landscape comes from a number of pollen diagrams. The later prehistoric clearance phase continued unchecked in many areas into the Roman era. Clearances attributed to this period have been noted in the Oldham area, at Cockerham and at Holcroft. In the central Rossendale area the clearance episode is estimated to have lasted from about 350 BC to AD 290. At Rusland Moss a clearance phase lasting for about five hundred years is bracketed by radiocarbon dates of 13 bc ± 50 and ad 589 ± 55. In all cases pollen representing both arable and pastoral cultivation has been recorded, and the general picture seems to have been one whereby small communities practised a mixed farming economy with perhaps a slight bias towards pastoralism.

The presence of the Roman army – and a maximum garrison of as many as 7,500 men has been suggested for the Pennines – must have fuelled demand for foodstuffs, and indeed for other commodities, clothing, leather footwear, etc. This in turn should have stimulated the growth of Romano-British rural settlement in the first and second centuries AD. In theory, each fort could have been sustained from its *territoria*, which, allowing for the terrain, need have been a zone of only 1 – 2 km radius around each fort.

In practice, it is likely that supplies were managed by levies on the region around each fort. As yet there is unsufficient evidence to show whether there was a close link between the siting of forts and native settlements. In the north-west of Cumbria, for example, forts seem to have been located to take advantage of pre-existing agricultural communities. Several farmsteads there are connected to each other and to forts by trackways. Forts in Lancashire seem to be more directly related to strategic considerations, guarding major crossing-points, Ribchester on the Ribble, Lancaster at the tidal limit of the Lune, Manchester at a central communication node. By their very nature such locations will tend to have acted as a focus for settlement, and they are eminently located to exploit the agricultural land flanking the river valleys.

Given this scenario, why did villa estates not develop to exploit the economic potential of the North-West? It was not because the region was too poor to support the villa economy and give a good return on investment. It is more likely that the region was considered too risky for the capital investment required. The North-West not only had an intensive military presence, but it was obviously seen as a military zone. It is true that a number of forts had been decommissioned during the second century, but the North-West remained firmly in military hands. The major supply bases at Wilderspool, Walton-le-Dale and perhaps Wigan (though excavations there are not conclusive) were probably run on quasi-military lines and there is no evidence that the pottery and tile kilns at Quernmore were anything other than military works servicing the fort at Lancaster.

Vici and industrial sites

The absence of villas helps to explain the development of vici, the civilian settlements attached to certain Roman forts. The rapid growth of vici outside north-western forts like Manchester, Ribchester and Lancaster has prompted the suggestion that they were deliberately encouraged, even planned, as satellite civilian settlements serving the needs of the garrisons and the Roman administration. As such they will have functioned as market-places where local farmers could have sold their produce to raise the money needed to meet their fiscal obligations under the Empire (taxes in kind only became the normal mode of collection in the later third century). It has been estimated that as much as a half of all produce was collected as tax or tribute under the native system of tribal chiefdoms. It is unlikely that the Romans will have taken less: in all probability they will have exacted rather more.

The *vici* did not only fulfil administrative and market functions. They will surely have had a social role, acting as a meeting-place where ideas and information as well as goods and money changed hands. The Manchester wordsquare, a fragment of amphora (pottery storage jar) inscribed with a piece of Latin doggere whose individual letters can be rearranged to form the words *Pater Noster* in the form of a cross, may have belonged to a merchant or other traveller who stayed at the *vicus* at Manchester in the 180s.

The Romans can therefore be credited with giving the North-West a taste of the cosmopolitan society that was Rome; with reintroducing the idea of centralised settlements based on forts; and also with giving the North-West its first, but by no means last, taste of large-scale industrial activity. Sometimes this industrial activity took place within the confines of the northern *vici*. At Manchester, which was probably the most important industrial *vicus* in the region, over thirty furnaces and smithing hearths (Pl. 6) were found during the course of rescue excavations in the 1970s (Jones 1974). *Vicus* activity was at its height after the Antonine re-garrisoning of the fort when imported iron blooms were fashioned into military equipment and tools, and hobnails for the soldiers' leather footwear.

To date none of the other north-western *vici* have yielded evidence for industrial activity on the scale of Manchester and it is clear that Manchester should be seen in the context of the industrial bases and supply depots which provisioned the army. The large industrial site at Wilderspool on the south bank of the Mersey across from Warrington produced metal goods, bronze as well as iron, glass, and pottery wares. Another major base operated at Walton-le-Dale on the southern bank of the Ribble. Both bases lie at the major crossing-points of their respective rivers. Walton lay at the tidal limit in Roman times; Wilderspool lay upriver on the Mersey but both it and Manchester were clearly accessible by barge. They were all well sited to take advantage of coastal routes for the bulk transport of heavy items like metalwork, pottery and raw materials.

Production at the supply bases was closely linked with military requirements. The kilns at Quernmore do not appear to have operated on any great scale after the second century, when there was a centralised pottery supply for the army. At Walton, after a possible hiatus in the mid-second century associated with the reduction in garrisons, the site was reorganised, perhaps to accommodate generalised storage buildings rather than workshops. There is no evidence for activity at Wigan beyond the third century and at Wilderspool the main phase of industrial activity ended around the third quarter of the second century. This may be linked with the withdrawal of most of the twentieth legion from Chester. There is some evidence for smaller-scale activity (perhaps after a break in occupation lasting until the mid-third century) which continued into the fourth century, but this seems to have been of an agricultural rather than industrial nature.

The viability of the *vici* was equally dependent on the needs of the garrison and administration. This helps to explain why the *vici* failed to develop into market centres once the garrisons departed. At Kirkham there is no evidence for sustained activity after the decommissioning of the fort in the second century. At Manchester the northern *vicus* was abandoned during the 140s in the absence of a garrison, though once the fort was recommissioned in the third quarter of the second century, the *vicus* again prospered.

The principal exception to this pattern occurs at Lancaster, where a substantial civilian settlement appears to have arisen during the second century. The excavators were themselves surprised by the scale of the civilian buildings on the Mitre Yard site which included a bath-house and a large courtyard building. The site showed evidence of four rebuilding phases. It has been suggested that the courtyard house was a residence of a grand scale, probably of an official nature (Jones and Shotter 1988: 277). The group of carvings unearthed at Burrow Heights a mile or so to the south of Lancaster sometime between 1794 and 1872 may be related to the occupancy of this residence. The four sculptured heads, headless human torso and two animals (?lions) are now (1990) on display in Lancaster Museum. They have been interpreted as part of a mausoleum sited outside the perimeter of the settlement in accordance with Roman law, along the main lowland route linking Lancaster with Walton-le-Dale and sites further south. This settlement continued to flourish throughout the third century despite a greatly reduced level of military activity. Indeed, there may not have been a garrison permanently in residence at the fort. Clearly the *vicus*, which began life in the late first century, had developed sufficiently to sustain itself. In part this reflects the rural prosperity of the whole Lune valley. The importance of Lancaster as a quasi-urban settlement after the late second century has also been tentatively associated with Severan reorganisation of the fleet, a detachment of which may have operated out of the top end of Morecambe Bay.

The Roman name for Lancaster is not known, but on the basis of an inscription found at Burrow, it has been suggested that the Lune area was known as *Contrebis* in Roman times (Shotter 1984) and that it functioned as a territorial unit within the Roman administrative system. Another major territorial division was arguably based on Ribchester. The legionary centurion who acted as commander of the Sarmatian cavalry unit stationed there after 175 also held the title *præpositus regionis*. Two holders of the office are known in the first half of the third century. Retired Sarmatian veterans were deliberately settled around Ribchester and it has been suggested that the region, which may have included the Fylde, was a centre for cavalry horses. This in itself, however, does not adequately explain the need to have an official of such high standing in the area.

It would be all too easy to carve up the North–West into such territories on the basis of known military sites, and to try to associate them with prehistoric and medieval territories. The Roman fort at Lancaster could be linked with the honour of Lancaster, via Tosti's estate of Halton (see Chapter 6). Ribchester could be linked with a territory either along the lower reaches of the Ribble and the Fylde, or with the middle reaches of the Ribble and its tributaries, perhaps with the strategic territory of Portfield, and with the de Lacy Honour of Clitheroe in the twelfth century AD. Such correlations, it must be recognised, are extremely simplistic. The locations of these military foci in the North-West, whether prehistoric, Roman or medieval, were all chosen to exploit the same strategic advantages, in particular to control routeways and crossing-points. Their dependent territories need have little in common, either in extent or organisation. On the other hand, the repeated selection of these strategic locations must have fostered certain traditions of land use and may well have encouraged some form of territorial identity and expectations.

The later Roman period

Later Roman Britain witnessed a growing regionalism, a break-down into multiple provinces. At the opening of the third century Britain had been partitioned into Britannia Superior and Britannia Inferior. Further divisions were made so that by the later fourth century there were five provinces where once there had been one. It has been argued that the fifth and latest province, Valentia, named after Valentinian and his brother Valens, encompassed north-west England. Chester and Carlisle have both been advanced as provincial capitals but neither has been widely accepted (Dornier 1982; Salway 1982: 411). There is still no certainty about the geographical location of Valentia and it seems safer to regard the Lancashire forts that were still in commission as being commanded from York.

Manchester, Ribchester and Lancaster were clearly occupied throughout most of the later period, though they suffered significant rebuilding and internal changes. This is especially marked at Lancaster which became a major coastal fort for the defence of the west coast against piratical attacks across the Irish Sea. Forts of this later period are chiefly remarkable for the physical strength of their defences: massive stone walls and bastions for artillery platforms; a reduced number of gates. The Wery Wall at Lancaster belongs to this late phase and is the remains of the defences of the fourth-century coastal station. The wall was first noticed by the sixteenth-century antiquarians Leland and Camden: the name 'Weary Wall' appears on Saxton's map of Lancashire of 1610. There has been a certain amount of controversy, especially over its alignment and date, but these issues have now been firmly settled by excavation and a date close to 326 has been confirmed by coin finds. Lancaster fits in well with the pattern of late Roman coastal defence works and can be compared with the surviving defences of the late coastal fort at Caer Gybi at Holyhead on Anglesey. There is epigraphic evidence for the presence of a detachment of *barcarii* or boatmen in the Lancaster area and Shotter suggests that they were stationed at Lancaster in the fourth century.

Other northern forts were garrisoned by *limitatenses*, poorly paid frontier troops who were often deployed in very small units. This reflects the recruitment difficulties experienced by the Roman administration during the third and fourth centuries. Despite a series of reorganisations of the army, by the fourth century the administration was forced to rely heavily on local recruiting for the army which tended to blur the distinctions between civilians and soldiers. The flow of pottery from the South comes to a halt after about 350. There was a slow fading of identifiably Roman aspects of life which served to increase regionalism and paved the way for further fragmentation in post-Romen times.

Few forts remained in commission beyond the 380s. Coin histograms have been used to argue the case for occupation at Lancaster and Manchester (as at Chester and Ravenglass). The situation at Ribchester is less clear and the absence of late coins leaves doubt that any garrison remained there. The *vici* had generally been abandoned much earlier. With the exception of Lancaster, *vicus* activity seems to have dwindled after *c*. 250.

The implications for the native population are not fully understood. Native sites that have been excavated tend to yield very little pottery or datable material. What pottery there is tends on the whole to belong to the first and second centuries. To date very few rural sites have produced unequivocally fourth-century material. One of these is Pilling (SD 411482), where pottery dated to after 370 was found together with animal bone, iron and glass during dredging of a stream called the Broadfleet. The context of this material has not been determined. One can only guess at the fate of the *vicani*, and of the workers at the supply bases. Unlike the Sarmatian veterans settled around Ribchester, there is no evidence that the *vicani* remained behind *en masse* in Lancashire to swell the native population. Presumably they departed in the wake of the garrisons.

Continuity and post-Roman settlement: central places in early Lancashire

Lancaster, Ribchester and Manchester, the three forts occupied until at least the 380s, have several features in common. One obvious common feature is their name: today they are all known by names ending in OE **c(e)aster**. The importance of Ribchester has waned in the last few centuries, whilst that of Manchester has increased tremendously, but all three are recorded in Domesday Book and they were places of at least local importance in the medieval period. It is significant that they are all sited to guard crossing-points of major rivers, the Lune, Ribble and Irwell. The continued importance of these crossings has enabled the three sites to act as 'central places' through much of the period covered by this book. The same tendency for former Roman sites to continue to act as a 'central place' can be observed at Walton-le-Dale and Wilderspool, again places located on major river crossings.

Crucial to these discussions is the whole concept of continuity. In the cases examined above there is no evidence for continuity of occupation, but there is evidence that the communication nodes continued to act as 'central place' after the Roman era. This term should not be confused with Christaller's 'Central Place Theory', borrowed from the nineteenth-century German economic geographer by archaeologists in an attempt to explain and predict distribution models for hillforts and towns in Roman Britain. 'Central Place Theory' has been used to predict the regular spacing of settlements within a closely defined settlement hierarchy. These settlements are ranked according to the range of functions or attributes associated with a particular place. Predictably, a few 'higher order' sites (like cities) are supported by many lesser sites (small market towns) which in turn rely on even smaller settlement sites (villages and hamlets). When 'central places' are mentioned in this book the reference is not to an ordered hierarchy of sites, though 'central places' will satisfy many of the criteria required of Christaller's higher order settlements. The term is instead being used to refer to locations which over time have continued to attract a high level of 'activity' (c.f. Grant 1986). This activity may take several forms, and it may be spread out over a rather loosely defined area – a kilometre square rather than an eight-figure grid reference.

Typically the central place will act as a focus for settlement, being an administrative, fiscal and/or military centre. By the historic period, if not before, central places will frequently have market functions and perhaps act as religious centres. In the case of Lancashire North of the Sands, access from the coast along river valleys to and from the Lake District central massif determined the siting of strategic central places. Further south, east-west routes from the coast across the Pennines were important, hence the location of central places controlling the crossing-places of the Lune, Ribble and Mersey. Different settlements acted as central places at different points of history. Wilderspool and Thelwall (Anglo-Saxon *burh*) lay on the south side of the Mersey; Warrington lay on the north bank. Walton-le-Dale and Penwortham (Norman motte and bailey) lay south of the Ribble; Preston grew up on the opposite bank. The territorial units (strategic territories) which supported these central places, and which were controlled from them, are important in understanding the evolution of territorial lordships in the North-West. Other central places developed within what may be described as resource territories (e.g. Kirkham and Treales; see below, Chapter 4). In these instances location depended less on control of communication routes and more on social and economic factors. In both cases, broader territorial and political factors influenced the precise siting of the settlements which held the controlling interest.

This interpretation of central place functioning provides a thread of continuity for the history of Lancashire. One must also have regard for the questions of continuity of settlement and continuity of both people and language. In the virtual absence of a documentary record for this period one would normally turn to the archaeological record.

No sites have yet been excavated which have been proved beyond doubt to have been used by the native British people during this era, a time which is usually referred to as the Early Christian period. So far no domestic site has been identified at all, though there are several possible religious sites. The best known of these is at Heysham, where St Patrick is reputed to have established a small chapel on the headland (Pl. 7). According to local tradition, St Patrick was shipwrecked off the Morecambe Bay coast sometime in the fifth century. Excavations at the site of the ruined Anglo-Saxon chapel on the headland in the late 1970s found no evidence for an Early Christian presence. Approximately 150 burials were found under the chapel floor and immediately outside the building but these have been provisionally assigned a ninth-century date, making them more or less contemporary with the upstanding stonework of the chapel. Nonetheless, there is good evidence from elsewhere in northern Britain for the sequence of early Christian oratory, through small eremetic monastery to medieval church. This apparently happened further north at Whithorn and such an explanation for Heysham would help to explain the ecclesiastical prominence of the place as attested by the number of pre-Norman carved stones and sculptured cross fragments. Whithorn developed into a coastal trading settlement and it would be reasonable to expect something similar at Heysham from where a ferry service still (1990) runs to the Isle of Man.

The rows of east-west aligned graves in the cemeteries discovered at Roosebeck (Lancashire North of the Sands) and Winwick have prompted suggestions that these were Early Christian burials, but there is no corroborative evidence. Roosebeck was only a small cemetery, of perhaps only seven graves, but at Winwick excavators in 1980 uncovered the remains of upwards of 600 grave slots, partly overlying a Bronze Age tumulus, at a site approximately 2 km from the parish church. No artefacts were found in the graves since the soil is very acid: little bone and no coffin material, if there was any, has survived (Freke 1982). East-west burials are not the sole prerogative of Christianity though elsewhere in the North prehistoric cemeteries tend to have a north-south alignment. Six hundred graves would represent the burials of a sizeable rural community over some generations and it may be that a different context for the graves should be sought (see Chapter 4).

Other Early Christian centres may be represented by churches with circular churchyards, though this is disputed by those who point to the curvilinear churchyard at Escomb (Durham) which apparently has an Anglo-Saxon origin. But the church in Bernicia was heavily influenced by missionary activity from Iona and the Celtic west. Thomas's study of Early Christain sites in north-west Britain (1971) lends credence to the theory of a pre-Saxon origin, and there are reasons for thinking that these circular enclosures may be the remains of Early Christian monastic communities. Many of our churches have suffered major rebuilding work over the centuries, and churchyard shape has often suffered as a result. Increased demand for burial space has also caused modification and churchyard extension. As a consequence one cannot always determine the original shape of the enclosure. There are, however, a number of instances where the enclosure is markedly circular; sometimes the road or street pattern has followed the circuit. Good examples include Eccles, Prescot, Melling (south-west Lancashire), Walton-on-the-Hill, Parbold, Halsall, Winwick and Pennington (North of the Sands). As will be shown, there is considerable, albeit circumstantial, evidence for the survival of

British communities in the North-West and one should be prepared to accept these sites as potential foci of early Christian activity.

The general scarcity and occasional unreliability of the archaeological data which is currently available, and especially the difficulties in establishing firm dates, mean that that it must be reinforced by other sources of evidence, such as place-names and environmental data.

Place-names

The use of place-names to elucidate settlement history is not without drawbacks. Caveats must be expressed concerning the difficulties in establishing a correct etymology for a name and concerning its likely date. One has to be aware that place-name study is an ongoing area of research: new interpretations and philosophies have come forward which have completely revised much of the work conducted before the 1960s. This revision primarily concerns the chronology of settlement names. A second revisionist movement is currently in progress as a new generation of theory has arisen to explain the significance of names for the nature and organisation of settlement and the landscape. A summary of current thinking is contained in the works of Margaret Gelling listed in the bibliography.

One or two general points can be made. In particular it must be appreciated that any distribution map, whether it purports to show British names or names used by the early Anglo-Saxons, is at best an incomplete record of the original distribution. The place-names of this country are a complex mixture of languages and dialects, and, indeed, of cultures. It is likely that over the millennia, the vast majority of our place-names have been lost. We know the names of hundreds of names from Roman Britain but only a small percentage has survived. Similarly, other names have gone out of currency as local circumstances have changed. Hamlets, villages and even whole counties have been swallowed up by suburban developments and administrative reorganisation. Domesday names like *Aschebi* (in the Myerscough area) and *Wibaldeslei* (in West Derby hundred) have been lost. West Derby and Amounderness were almost certainly renamed by Scandinavian speakers, as were a large number of settlements which now also bear Scandinavian names. Other names are relative newcomers on the map. Even today new names are coined, like 'Red Rose', proposed for the Central Lancashire New Town development in the early 1970s and taken up as the name of the local radio station. Other names have been more successful, like Nelson and Fleetwood which arose in the nineteenth century, the one from an inn in Marsden named after Lord Nelson, the other being named after Sir Peter Hesketh-Fleetwood who founded the town. The degree of stability now apparent in our place-names is a relatively recent feature induced by bureaucratic inertia.

A second point is that many early place-names were essentially topographical terms. They were coined as the names of features in the natural landscape: hills, rivers, open land, etc. Some topographical names were widely used as regional names and cannot easily be depicted on a distribution map by a single location. The Lyme is a good example. The name has been derived from the British *lēmo, 'an elm', and can be taken to mean 'the district of the elm'. The name has survived in several modern place-names, including Newcastle-under-Lyme and Ashton-under-Lyne. It seems to have referred to the Pennine uplands on the south-east border of Lancashire, the east and south-east borders of Cheshire, and the northern borders of Staffordshire and Shropshire. In the records of the counties and palatinates of Lancaster and Chester the regional name is used as a boundary term to refer to the limits of palatine jurisdiction. Makerfield, a hybrid name meaning 'the open land by/near the masonry walling', is another regional name which has survived as an affix for townships around Wigan.

One must also have regard for the forms in which names have survived. Very few British names have survived intact. Besides total loss, replacement of all or part of a name by a direct equivalent in another language (translation) may have occurred. It is difficult to give a definite example from Lancashire but Bede provides several instances of a dual-naming tradition where British names seem to have existed side by side with their English equivalents. Chester, according to Bede (HE, II, 2), was called *Legacestir* by the English and *Carlegion* by the Britons. Bede commonly gives the translation of a place-name into Latin. This prompts the suggestion that some names were translated from British into Latin and thence to English through the intermediary of the church (HE. I. i), rather than directly from British to

English by bilingual native communities. Indeed, though it is usually stated that the English had borrowed Latin **castra** (>OE **c(e)aster**) whilst still on the Continent, *Legacestir* may be an Anglicisation of the Latin name for the 'City of the Legion'.

Besides translation, instances occur where there is replacement by a word which has a similar sound but a different meaning. This is probably what has happened in the case of Penwortham. The first syllable of the name clearly derives from British **penno**, Old Welsh **penn**, terms meaning 'a hill' or, when used adjectivally, 'chief, top of'. The last part of the name is the Old English word **hām** for 'a village' or 'an estate'. The medial syllable, ostensibly another Old English word, **worð** meaning 'an enclosure', is very likely a substitution for what had become an unintelligible British word. Not surprisingly, the Norman–French Domesday scribe garbled the name, entering it as *Peneverdant*, thereby giving the name a temporary French flavour.

Various hybrid forms occur. The first part of the Roman name for Manchester, *Mamucium*, has survived compounded with **ceaster**; Old English elements like **hām** and **tūn** are found with British elements in Cheetham (Primitive Welsh **cēd*) and Eccleston (Primitive Welsh **eglēs*). Makerfield in another hybrid name. All of these examples are names where an English element has been added to a word borrowed from the British language. Eccleston is the 'settlement of/belonging to/at the church'. Sometimes a British river name, like Cocker, has given rise to a settlement name, in this case Cockerham. Here we have what might be called a 'transferred' place-name, the pre-existing British river name being employed with the addition of Old English **hām** to give an English name indicating the location of the settlement. Another example is Darwen, where the town is named after the British-named river. Some hybrid names appear to be tautological: an explanatory element has been added to an existing name with a forgotten, though presumably identical meaning. Ths classic example is, of course, Pendle, where the Old English word **hyll** has been suffixed to the British term for a hill. Further explanation became necessary to distinguish between the hill and the nearby settlement, hence Pendle Hill and Pendleton.

In all a total of over fifity names containing pre-English elements can be identified (Fig. 3.1). This is almost certainly an underestimate which will be revised upwards once a more comprehensive study of all the minor names in the county has been

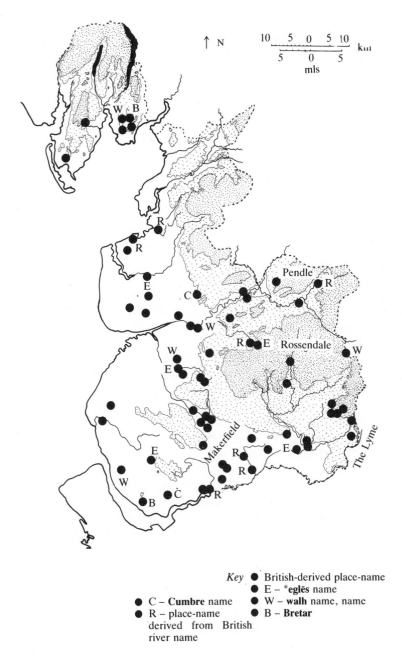

Fig. 3.1 British place-names in Lancashire

completed, along the lines of the English Place-Name Society's Cheshire survey. The virtual absence of settlement or habitative names – Treales, 'township of the court', is a rare exception – was once taken to mean that the native British settlements had all been wiped out. It is now realised that topographical terms were widely used both as regional names and to name early settlements and estates. These topographical names include the names of rivers like the Lune, Cocker and Douglas; hill names like Pendle, and names like Penketh, Culcheth and Tulketh, which all refer to woods.

Place-names and the British landscape

River names, or hydronymics, are particularly resistant to change. Indeed, it has been suggested that some of our river names, the name of the River Wyre for example, go back even further than Celtic times and belong to an earlier generation of languages (Nicholaisen 1982). Rivers are an obvious feature in the landscape; like hills they are fixed, unchanging (allowing for minor deviations in the course of a river) points of reference. Woods are less permanent but were still regarded as enough of a fixture to be accepted as signposts in the landscape. Over time these wood names became transferred to nearby settlements. it is noticeable that some of the British wood names, those in *cęd, lie near to English names signifying wooded area. Culcheth lies next to the parish of Leigh which includes West Leigh, Astley, Tyldesley and Shakerley, all names derived from OE *lēah, a term with woodland connotations (see Chapter 4). Tulketh, on the outskirts of Preston, lies between Lea and Fulwood. This hints at a certain continuity in the physical appearance of the landscape from British to Anglo-Saxon times, and perhaps at a continuity of land-use.

This argument for continuity cannot be stretched too far, however. Whilst there is no suggestion that the Romano-British opening-up of the landscape continued everywhere unabated, it is possible that in some localities, especially in southern Lakeland, the clearance episode did not peak until after the fourth century. Pennington (1970) links the clearances shown by pollen diagrams from some of the Morecambe Bay mosses with a radiocarbon date of 460 ±100ad. The clearance phase noted at Rusland Moss continued until around 589 ±55ad.

Elsewhere, however, clearances had peaked much earlier. Pollen diagrams from many other sites in the North-West confirm that Romano-British clearances were succeeded by a period of extensive woodland regeneration. At Cockerham, the clearance phase was soon followed by a regeneration episode which is estimated to have lasted for a couple of hundred years over the fifth and sixth centuries (Oldfield and Statham 1965). Deposits from Deep Clough in Rossendale Forest have been interpreted as showing that woodland there regained Bronze Age levels: 80 per cent of pollen in the samples was arboreal (Tallis and McGuire 1972). In other places the regeneration was less complete though still marked. In the Oldham area, for example, some arable and pastoral activity continued for a while (Tallis 1964). Pollen indicative of arable cultivation then ceased and pastoral indicators dropped to half their previous values. At Holcroft, flanking the lower Mersey, agricultural activity was only sustained at greatly reduced levels (Birks 1965). It might be argued that these pollen records from mosses are biased towards the poorer quality land, marginal soils which would be most vulnerable and so most likely to experience regeneration. This may be true; nonetheless they do indicate a reversal of the trend of previous centuries which had seen a widespread opening-up of the landscape for agricultural purposes.

The exact dating of the regeneration is open to question. Apparently it varied from place to place. At Rusland regeneration did not take place until after 589 ±55ad. In central Rossendale Tallis and McGuire have estimated that regeneration began much earlier, after around AD 290. At Wessenden near Oldham, regeneration is linked to the general post-Roman recurrence of peat growth. A similar picture of partial but non-synchronous woodland regeneration has been observed in many parts of Britain, but most markedly on marginal terrain.

What are the implications of this picture of woodland regeneration? It is tempting to generalise and to see this as an indication of the gradual abandonment of former arable and pastures consequent upon the progressive demilitarisation of the North-West. Marginal land is likely to have been soonest and most seriously affected. Other factors will have contributed to this retreat from the margins. The generally unsettled times, the breakdown of the economy nationally after the late fourth century, and the worsening weather would all have influenced decisions on the part of farmers to retrench. These factors could have contributed to a reduction in population levels. There is no direct evidence, but it is widely accepted that there was a period of demographic decline in the North-West after the fourth century. Outbreaks of plague are recorded amongst the British population in the middle years of the sixth century. Welsh and Irish annals refer to the resulting *mortalitas magna*. Morris (1973) has claimed that this was bubonic plague (*Pasteurella pestis*), brought back from the east by traders using the East Mediterranean–Atlantic sea routes in the 540s. Not all scholars accept this, however, and suggest other infections. Its impact on the native population is also a matter of some debate. Certainly the plague did not cause the reduced population levels, though it may have hindered demographic recovery.

British kingdoms

One must not lose sight of the evidence for post-Roman clearances which are evidenced around the northern end of Morecambe Bay. Late clearances are not confined to southern Lakeland. Pollen diagrams from White Moss in Craven demonstrate that there was a change there from sporadic, low-intensity agricultural activity to a pattern of comprehensive woodland clearances for more intensive agricultural use around 480 ±100ad (I. P. Jones 1976). These clearances may be linked with a revival of the fortunes of native dynasties, or with the establishment *ab initio* of new native dynasties and territorial lordships.

During the fifth and sixth centuries a number of small British kingdoms came into existence in the western and northern parts of Britain. Urien of Rheged and other rulers of these successor states are known to us through the medium of oral tradition, some of which was being written down by the ninth century, if not earlier. A critical reinterpretation of the material has challenged the veracity of some of these traditions, and the picture which emerges is far from consistent. In some places the British kingdoms are obviously broadly based on earlier Romano-British territories. In the North-West, the kingdom of Rheged succeeded the *civitas Carvetiorum* which was presumably centred on Carlisle. An attempt has been made to identify the Old English name for

Rochdale, *Recedham*, with Rheged, but this does not stand up on etymological grounds.

Other British kingdoms ringing Lancashire can be identified. Faull (Faull and Moorhouse 1981) has proposed a kingdom based on Craven, a region where there was considerable agricultural activity around the fifth century ad. The natural boundaries of such a kingdom would give a resource base similar to that of the prehistoric territory focused on the hillfort at Ingleborough. To the south of Craven lay Elmet, one of the few reliably documented British kingdoms, which was absorbed into the English kingdom of Northumbria after 617. Elmet lay to the east of the Pennines, focused on Leeds. It extended from Craven to the Don, and its eastern boundary along the belt of magnesian limestone has been mapped using the evidence of British place-names and those like Barwick in Elmet and Sherburn in Elmet which retain the territorial affix (Faull 1980).

Efforts to identify the small kingdoms on the Lancashire side of the Pennines have met with little success. An attempt has been made to locate the lost kingdom of Teyrnllwg with north-west England, for example, but this is not widely accepted (VCH II: 175; Bu'lock 1956). The surviving distribution of British place-names, and of names incorporating British-related elements, may offer some clues to the possible identification of areas of lordship, but it must be emphasised that the distribution is only one of survival, not necessarily an analogue of the orginal distribution.

As Fig. 3.1 shows, there are several small concentrations of names. One major grouping can be found in the Wigan area, extending into the later hundreds of Leyland and Newton down to the Mersey. These include Brynn, Haskayne, Ince, Pemberton, Ulnes Walton, Eccleston, Culcheth and Penketh, plus the river names Yarrow and Douglas. Makerfield and perhaps Wigan itself have British antecedents. A second group can be identified in the Fylde: Preese and Preesall, Great and Little Eccleston and Inskip. In the Greater Manchester area there are two small groups of British names, a group of hybrids on the valley floor: Manchester, Cheetham and Cheetwood, Pendleton and Pendlebury; and a group with a high proportion of British topographical names on the edge of Rossendale Forest around Oldham including Werneth, Glodwick and Croichlow. The first part of the name Rossendale is

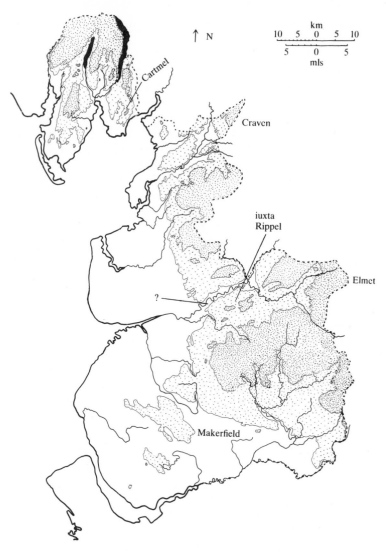

Fig. 3.2 Possible British lordships in the North-West

derivde from the diminutive form of the British name for a moor, which becomes Welsh **rhos**.

These names fall into loosely defined geographical regions and are associated with areas of better quality land. The Wigan group can be associated with the belt of higher, relatively fertile and well drained land on the edge of the south-west Lancashire mossland belt. This corridor of 'high' land was utilised by the Romans for their road from Wilderspool to Walton-le-Dale. Further north, Preese and Inskip are obviously linked to the Fylde Ridge, an arc of high ground above the Fylde mosses. The names around Manchester fall within the Manchester embayment, a clearly marked lowland entity demarcated by Pennine foothils. Settlements located in these lowlands may well have used the uplands around Oldham for seasonal grazing.

It is possible that these groups of names have survived in natural resource territories which formed the basis of British lordships and, ultimately, Anglo-Saxon territorial units (Fig. 3.2). The hybrid regional name Makerfield could conceivably have been given to name a pre-existing British lordship centred on Ashton, Ince and Newton. Similarly, the eleventh-century hundred named after Salford may represent another earlier territorial unit. The British place-names of the Fylde fall within the landed unit called Amounderness after the 930s when its southern boundary ran along the Ribble. Several scholars believe that the grant of lands *iuxta Rippel* (literally 'near the Ribble') to the Northumbrian church at Ripon in the 670s included the Fylde (see Chapter 4). This is far from conclusive, however, for the lands referred to could have been further inland along the central reaches of the Ribble. Indeed, a good case could be made out for the Ribble–Whalley area, especially in view of the postulated early minster church at Whalley which had workshops producing carved stone crosses in the pre-Norman period. Even if the lower reaches are meant, one cannot be certain that the land, and presumably the lordship, was confined to the north bank of the river. Bispham place-names (literally 'bishop's estate') are known from both Amounderness and Leyland hundred. It may be that *iuxta Rippel* was in origin a small British kingdom or lordship encompassing the west Lancashire lowlands on either side of the Ribble, as far south as Makerfield, and extending into the Pennine foothills above Whalley. But while the extent of the lands *iuxta Rippel* are debatable, the real significance of the grant is that it was referring to a recognisable territorial unit.

Further north, the naturally defined territories based on the Furness and Cartmel peninsulas may also have been recognisable lordships in pre-Saxon times. When the king of Northumbria endowed the community of St Cuthbert with Cartmel 'and all the Britons with it' in the 670s, the gift was manifestly one of a landed unit with rights of lordship over the local population.

British place-names are absent from some parts of the map, especially around Liverpool and the south-west Lancashire coast, and along the Lune valley. This should not be taken to signify that these areas were uninhabited in post-Roman centuries, or that they did not fall within any British kingdom or lordship. It is a reflection of the intensity of changes in place-name structure during the Anglo-Saxon and Scandinavian eras.

Precisely what these territorial units were is difficult to determine. Some authors refer to them as estates but this probably implies too organised a system, with overtones of central management of landed resources and tenurial structures binding the population in a landlord–tenant relationship. It is unlikely that estates as such had existed in the North-West either in Roman times or in the centuries immediately after. One should perhaps envisage these territories as lordships, as areas of monopolistic use and loosely defined bundles of rights. The kingdoms comprised of these lordships were not kingdoms in the modern sense of the term either. The idea of kingship evolved very slowly and initially these British 'kings' were often little more than war leaders. On analogy with the situation in Ireland and Scotland, it is likely that these kings exerted a form of overlordship over their kingdom by exacting tribute; demonstrating their military power and supplementing their wealth by raiding other kingdoms and even by slave-trading. According to his own account, St Patrick was captured by Irish slave-traders in the fifth century, but the Irish were not the only ones involved in this lucrative activity.

The arguments linking concentrations of British and British-related place-names to areas of territorial lordship between the fifth and seventh centuries are admittedly rather tenuous. Nevertheless they give a framework for the development of society and territorial exploitation in the North-West. The names of the British kingdoms lying to the west of the Pennines are not known,

but one can be sure that the North-West was not a territorial vacuum. Small kingdoms comprising one or more territorial groupings or lordships evolved there during this period. Over time these
lordships will have developed into landed estates exploiting the
landscape on an organised basis. This was a slow development,
reflecting the low level of rural productivity of this part of England. The material poverty of the rural population did, however,
guarantee the survival of its national identity and native language
into the seventh century and beyond. The takeover of Lancashire
was not high on the Anglo-Saxon agenda, and the Anglo-Saxons
did not become seriously involved there until two or three hundred
years had elapsed since they first set foot on English soil.

4

Lancashire under the
Anglo-Saxons

Outline history

A bare outline of events following upon the *Adventus Saxonum* can be reconstructed by reference to various pre-Conquest documentary sources. One has to bear in mind, however, that much early material is extraordinarily suspect, even unhistorical. These sources are also geographically biased and very subjectively written. Bede, the principal source for the early history of Northumbria, was writing about the English Church as he knew it from his 'Roman' monastery of Jarrow in Northumbria. He was hostile to the British church which had caused so much trouble over the dates of Easter and about the correct form of tonsure. Bede provides a detailed description of the slaughter of the British monks of Bangor-on-Dee at the hands of Northumbrians after the Battle of Chester which took place between 613 and 616. Bede complacently notes that this was a fulfilment of a prophecy made by St Augustine when the seven British bishops refused to recognise his authority and adopt 'the Roman customs of the universal church'. Augustine prophesied 'that the faithless Britons, who had rejected the offer of eternal salvation, would incur the punishment of temporal destruction' (HE II, 2). Elsewhere there are glimpses of how the early history of the English was rewritten in order to legitimise new authorities. The *Anglo-Saxon Chronicle* therefore reinterprets Augustine's prophecy, blaming the warmongering Britons for the Battle of Chester: 'If the Welsh refuse peace with us, they shall perish at the hands of the Saxons.' The account is, therefore, essentially hagiographical and should not be taken at face value.

The eastern and south-eastern parts of the country had been brought under Anglo-Saxon control during the fifth century, but this had little direct impact on the North-West. Gradually, during the sixth century, the English kingdoms of Mercia and Northumbria appear. Mercia, the kingdom of the mark or boundary, presumably in recognition of its position in relationship to British kingdoms, first emerged in the Trent valley. It soon encompassed other communities across the Midlands including the *Pecsæte* and the *Wreocensæte*. In the North-East Northumbria was another loose grouping of smaller units. It comprised a number of British kingdoms and, by the second half of the century, two Anglo-Saxon ones, Deira based on the Wolds, and Bernicia further north. By the end of the sixth century the Anglo-Saxons had absorbed the native kingdoms of the north east and in 617 Edwin annexed the small British Pennine kingdom of Elmet.

The ascendancy of strong Northumbrian rulers and the opportunities afforded by power struggles between the rival Northumbrian dynasties brought the two large Anglo-Saxon kingdoms of Northumbria and Mercia into violent conflict. Religious differences counted for little in the political manoeuvring of the seventh century. The heathen Mercians under Penda allied themselves with the Christian rulers of Gwynedd and Powys, an alliance which endured despite several bloody battles. One of the greatest successes for the Mercian–Welsh alliance took place in 642 when the alliance defeated Oswald of Northumbria at the Battle of *Maserfelth*. The exact site of this battle is unknown. Formerly it was believed to have been in the Oswestry area (Gelling 1989), but there is a strong tradition linking Oswald's last battle with the Makerfield area of Lancashire, and in particular with the church of St Oswald at Winwick (Hulton 1853). The place-name evidence is not conclusive but there are obvious superficial similarities between *Maserfelth* and Makerfield. *Maserfelth* is Bede's name for the battle; a Welsh poem associated with the *Canu Heledd* cycle refers to it as *Maes Cogwy*. It is called *Bellum Cocboy* in other Welsh sources. This name recalls the Romano-British name *Coccium*, usually identified with the Roman site at Wigan, a little to the north of Winwick. Prehistoric tumuli in the vicinity have been claimed as the burial places of Oswald and his men, but they will surely have been accorded a Christian burial. The substantial cemetery excavated at Winwick (discussed in the previous chapter) is a more suitable candidate.

Relations between the two Anglo-Saxon kingdoms remained strained until Penda's demise; overlordship swung in favour of first one and then the other kingdom's ruling dynasty. Marriage alliances as well as battles played a part in this. Finally, after the Battle of Trent in 678, a peace formula was agreed through the intervention of archbishop Theodore. In the words of Bede: 'The peace thus made was maintained between these kings and their peoples for many years' (HE IV, 21). It is generally accepted that Northumbria's southern limits were defined by this accord. To the west of the Pennines the southern boundary was no doubt fixed along the Mersey. The name itself is derived from an Old English term meaning 'boundary river' and its coining surely belongs to this period when it formed the boundary between two English-speaking kingdoms, even if it had already long been a boundary of the highest status.

Arguments based on historical probability and place-name evidence for the use of the Mersey as Northumbria's south-western boundary are strengthened by archaeological evidence. The Nico Ditch, a linear earthwork lying in the eastern suburbs of Manchester, has been assigned to this phase by Hart (1977). He suggests that it is part of a frontier work thrown up or refurbished by the Northumbrians in the seventh century. Such earthworks are notoriously difficult to date but the Nico Ditch may relate to defensive dykes of the Aberford Dyke system thrown up on the eastern side of the Pennines. The location of these eastern dykes is consistent with the defence of the kingdom of Elmet (Faull and Moorhouse 1981) against the Anglo-Saxons in the early seventh century. Ramm (unpublished lecture), however, suggests that the south-west-facing Beca Bank was a Northumbrian construction against the Mercians. It is unlikely that these dykes will ever be satisfactorily dated. Nonetheless, the existence of the Nico Ditch confirms the significance of the Mersey mossland belt as a political and military boundary.

The Mersey mosses had acted as a frontier in earlier centuries when they formed the border zone between the Brigantes and the Cornovii, and between *Britannia Secunda* and *Flavia Caesarensis*.

To some extent there will still have been a frontier zone rather than a single definitive line, but over time the zone narrowed until it became fixed on the river itself. This progressive definition was encouraged by the communication system. The pervasive influence of the Roman road network should not be underestimated. In the North-West these roads continued in use for long after the departure of the Roman army. Their importance lies in the way they stabilised the few crossing-points across rivers like the Mersey. Runcorn Gap afforded a tidal crossing, and a more important crossing lay inland where the Roman road crossed the river from Wilderspool to Warrington. Further inland still, there are several crossing-places which increased in importance in later Saxon and medieval times. At Stockport, for example, again presumably where the Roman road(s) crossed the river, a trading centre (or **port**) grew up at the crossing-place.

The significance of the arrangements made after the Battle of Trent is not limited to the fixing of Northumbria's boundary with Mercia. There is an implicit recognition that the British kingdoms of north-west England were, by the end of the 670s, firmly under the control of the ruling dynasty of the English kingdom of Northumbria. There may have been infiltration and perhaps some small-scale settlement before the Northumbrians gained political control to the west of the Pennines, but this has left little trace.

Archaeological remains of the pagan Anglo-Saxons

There is scant evidence to indicate that there was a significant Anglo-Saxon presence in Lancashire before the middle decades of the seventh century. This is some two hundred years or so after the arrival of the Anglo-Saxons in the south and east of England. The nature and extent of the Anglo-Saxon settlement of Lancashire is, not surprisingly, very different in character from that found elsewhere in the country. This is illustrated most graphically by the surviving archaeological remains of the pagan Anglo-Saxon period, that is, those which can be assigned a date before *c*. 650. Meaney (1964) lists only four possible Lancashire sites in her gazetteer of early Anglo-Saxon burials published in 1964. These are the reported burials at Crossmoor near Inskip in the Fylde, and Hasty Knoll near Blackrod; the reported pagan period pottery vessel from Red Bank near Victoria Railway Station in

Manchester; and the group of pagan period grave goods from Ribchester Museum.

Close examination of the reports of the discoveries does little to validate the finds as evidence for pagan Anglo-Saxon activity in Lancashire. With the exception of the Ribchester material, the grave goods have all been lost since their discoveries in the eighteenth and nineteenth centuries. From their descriptions, the finds from Crossmoor and Hasty Knoll are not conclusively Anglo-Saxon. The Ribchester material is unequivocally pagan Anglo-Saxon but entirely without provenance. The closest affinities for the finds are grave goods from East Anglia, and excavations by the Cumbria and Lancashire Excavation Unit have failed to find any trace of a possible Anglo-Saxon cemetery in the area. The Red Bank urn, which is a little later than the Ribchester vessels, was found in 1850 on one of the approaches to the rear of Victoria Station in Manchester. The provenance of the urn is generally accepted despite its apparent isolation. The relationship, if any, with the rather enigmatic features interpeted as four Anglo-Saxon sunken-floored huts (*grubenhäuser*) excavated at the other end of Manchester, has yet to be established. These features were excavated just outside the north gate of the Roman fort at Manchester which lies about a mile away from Victoria Station at the opposite end of Deansgate. The 'huts', which range in area from $3 \cdot 2 \, \text{m} \times 2 \cdot 0 \, \text{m}$ to $6 \cdot 4 \, \text{m} \times 2 \cdot 5 \, \text{m}$, had an associated cobbled 'yard' surface. They were cut through the upper layers of the northern exit road from the fort and through the fill of the late Roman ditches. Stratigraphically, the features must postdate the ditches which contain late fourth-century pottery sherds in their fill. The 'huts' have been loosely dated to the fifth to tenth centuries and may represent some sort of squatter occupation on the part of a small group of wandering Anglo-Saxons (Walker 1986).

Meaney's group of four possible pagan burials cannot be accepted as very secure evidence for the actual presence of Anglo-Saxons in Lancashire. Some further evidence has come to light since she produced her gazetteer but it does little to fill out the general picture. The most significant of the recent finds is the 'canoe burial' found on the township boundary of Quernmore, just to the south-east of Lancaster. The burial was discovered during the construction of a new car park by the Jubilee Tower, a local beauty spot on the moors overlooking the Lune estuary and Morecambe Bay. The coffin consisted of two large pieces of oak, both shaped like canoes and apparently fashioned from the same tree. Acids from the peat layer which covered the coffin had destroyed all trace of the body except for hair, finger and toe nails. The woven woollen shroud also survived. At the time of writing the burial is on display at Lancaster Museum. Initially it was believed to be a Bronze Age find but radiocarbon dating of wood from the coffin yielded radiocarbon ages of 1,340 ±110 (Birm 430) and 1,300 ±100 (Birm 474). When calibrated to give a calendar date (Klein *et al.* 1982), the age of the wood from which the coffin was made lies somewhere between AD 545/580 and 895/900 (95 per cent confidence level).

The scarcity of archaeological material attributable to the pagan Anglo-Saxons is only partly due to the low levels of population and material wealth. There is no reason to suspect that there ever was a large wave of Anglo-Saxon immigrants in the North-West. This is not the only reason, however, and it may be that pagan Saxons were frequently buried in existing Christian churchyard cemeteries.

Place-names

The archaeological data can be supplemented by reference to the group of place-names which are accepted as belonging to this first phase of Anglo-Saxon activity in Lancashire. In the previous chapter reference was made to the British names; here the English names coined before about AD 700 will be considered. As noted in Chapter 3, over the past three decades there have been major changes in place-name studies. Older theories concerning the chronology of English place-names have been revised and a new sequence of development put forward. Work on the meaning and significance of elements, especially topographical terms for common landscape themes, has opened up new avenues for further exploration.

Place-names in singular **ing** (often used as a river or hill name) and **hām** ('an estate, a village'), including names in the combination -**inghām**, underpin the new chronological scheme. They, together with simple topographical place-names like Salford, 'willow ford', and Blackburn, 'black stream', form the basis of the currently accepted chronology of early English place-names which has superseded the chronology based on plural **ingas**, pagan place-names and archaic personal names. This is a major new departure which has profound implications for the interpretation of the whole nature of the Anglo-Saxon settlement of the country. No longer is the invasion and settlement dominated by groups of eponymous tribal or kinship groups, the 'xingas', who were thought to have given their names to settlements like Reading and Hastings. Furthermore, many of the early **hām**-named settlements have an apparently close relationship with former Romano-British settlements. Far from shunning Roman sites as the 'work of giants', the early Anglo-Saxons seem to have settled in and around the pre-existing settlement structure in the southern and midland counties of England.

One must now consider how these new interpretations apply to the north-west of England. The early English names occurring in Lancashire South of the Sands are discussed in the *Journal of the English Place-Name Society* (volume 18), where their etymologies are discussed in detail. The names which primarily concern us here are Abram, Bispham (2x), Cheetham, Cockerham, Heysham, Higham, Kirkham, Penwortham, *Recedham* (former name of Rochdale), Tatham and Thornham; Gressingham, Habergham, Padiham, Whittingham; names in Billinge including Billington, Bryning, Melling (2x), Staining; Blackburn, Burn, Burnage (?), Burnley, Golborne, Downham, Quarlton (from **dūn**, 'hill'), Smithdown, Livesey, Cantsfield, Hundersfield, Makerfield, Carnforth, Salford and Scotforth. To these may be added three more names from North of the Sands, Aldingham, Bardsea and Walney. The names are shown in Fig. 4.1. The distribution of these names, like the distribution of the British names, is not a comprehensive one. Some early names have surely been lost, replaced, or transformed out of recognition. Kirkham, for example, shows the influence of the Scandinavian word **kirkja** which has gradually replaced the Old English **cirice**, 'church'. The Domesday name *Recedham* has been replaced by Rochdale. In the case of Thornham (Middleton parish) and Gressingham, endings in **tūn** and **hām** appear as short-lived alternatives.

When we look at the group of 12 **hām** and 5 **inghām** names one or two interesting facts emerge. There are both upland and lowland examples but overall there is a marked preponderance of riverine and coastal locations (Fig. 4.1). Aldingham, Bispham

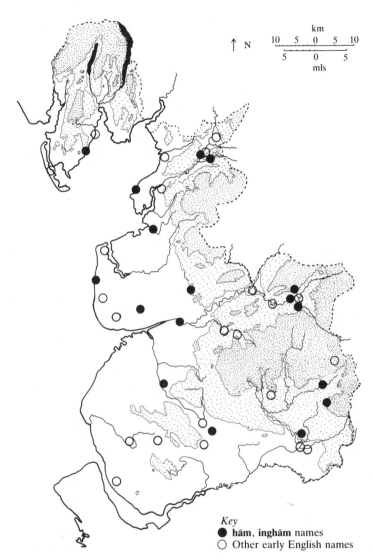

Fig. 4.1 Early English place-names in Lancashire

(Fylde), Heysham, Cockerham and Penwortham lie either on the coast or at the lowest crossing-points of rivers and can be contrasted with Padiham on the Calder valley bottom and nearby Higham and Habergham; and with Rochdale (*Recedham*) on the River Roch and nearby Thornham. Gressingham and Tatham lie along the flood plains formed by the Lune and its tributaries. It is possible that there has been some confusion between **hām** and the topographical term **hamm** which would be apposite for such topographical locations, but it is unlikely that this has been the case with every name cited. This **hām** distribution reflects the importance of access not only to drinking water and to good agricultural land, but also to the communications network. This network had been formalised by the Romans who had constructed roads to link the garrisons stationed along the major natural routeways. The coastal routes were important, too, and in Roman times it was possible to travel from North Wales via Chester, Walton-le-Dale and Lancaster to the Solway and beyond by hugging the coast and sailing from one estuary to the next. The persistent survival of the beachhead trading site at Meols on the Wirral peninsula testifies to the continued importance of the coastal route. Meols was a centre for trade across the Irish Sea with Ireland, as well as with the rest of Britain, from at least Roman times. This trade continued through the fifth, sixth and seventh centuries right into the Anglo-Scandinavian period. Though it cannot be proved, there must be a suspicion that Heysham, or somewhere close by, had a similar function. Hints of a link with the Atlantic–East Mediterranean trade routes of the fourth to seventh centuries are given by the sherd of African slipware (not later than fourth century; Bird 1977) and the reports of Byzantine coins found 'in the river area' at Lancaster.

It is also relevant that so many of the **hām**-named settlements became ancient parish centres. South of the Sands, 50 per cent of the **hāms**, including Penwortham, Heysham and Rochdale (*Recedham*), had this status by the 1290s, compared with less than 16 per cent of the **tūns**. The pattern is repeated in Lancashire North of the Sands.

There are fewer instances where **ing** is used as a major settlement name without the addition of **hām**, though Billing(e), a descriptive hill name, occurs several times. The first part of the name derives from Old English words referring to the shape of the hill, OE **bill**, **bile**, **belle**, respectively 'a bill, a sword, a sharp ridge', 'a bill, a beak, a narrow promontory', 'a bell, a bell-shaped hill'. On its own the distribution of this group of place-names is not very informative, but when mapped together with names in **hām**, **inghām**, it can be seem that they tend to occur in the same general areas, i.e. along the Lune valley, in the Fylde and in south-west Lancashire.

Topographical names form a larger group. They can be rather difficult to identify with precision since some of the name-forming elements, especially **feld** and **ford**, enjoyed a long currency. It has been necessary to limit the discussion to major settlement names documented by 1212. The Domesday Survey, although by no means a comprehensive gazetteer of settlements in existence by 1086, provides a reasonable list of major place-names north of the Ribble. Unfortunately there is no comparable survey of major names in Lancashire south of the Ribble before King John's Inquest of 1212. The distribution of topographical elements broadly follows the pattern set by the other early names. There is a marked attraction for riverine locations but this is hardly surprising bearing in mind the number of **ford**, **burna** and **ēg** names like Salford, Blackburn and Bardsea. The upland **feld** names, Cantsfield in the north and Hundersfield in the south-east of the county, also call for comment. They should not be viewed in isolation for they form part of a longer chain which includes Dukinfield, Macclesfield and, on other side of Pennines, Huddersfield, Sheffield, Chesterfield, and so on. The term **feld** in these names refers to the upland moors which were probably used for common pasture in the early centuries of the Anglo-Saxon era (Gelling 1984).

Only one of the early **ing**-named settlements, Melling in the Lune valley, had acquired parish status by the 1290s. Similarly, topographical names do not figure largely in parish lists. Blackburn is a rare exception and it should be noted that Blackburn and Salford were hundred names in the eleventh century.

Overlap between English and British place-names

Perhaps the most significant aspect about the distribution of early English place-names is the way that their distribution overlaps with the distribution of British names (Fig. 3.1). In both cases

D

there are small concentrations in south-west Lancashire, in the Manchester embayment, along the Ribble and its tributaries, along the Fylde Ridge, and to a lesser extent in Lancashire North of the Sands. The intimate relationship between English and British names on the ground is reflected in the composition of the place-names themselves and, indeed, contributes to the appearance of overlap throughout the county. Several of these place-names are in fact hybrid names sharing a British and an English element. In Cockerham, a river name of British derivation is found with **hām**; Cheetham has **hām** combined with a British term meaning 'wood'. In the regional name Makerfield, Old English **feld** occurs with a British word meaning 'masonry', 'walling', which is ultimately derived from Latin; and Penwortham seems to have **hām** suffixed on an unidentified British name.

What is the significance of these hybrid names? They are all essentially English names used by English speakers even though they are making use of non-English elements. This borrowing is most marked in the hybrid examples where pre-existing British names like *Mamucium* are Anglicised into Manchester, etc. But the borrowing did not stop with hybrid forms. Over time other purely British names were assimilated by English – and Scandinavian – speakers. It is presumed that the assimilation took place over a lengthy period. One reason for this is the presence of a number of unintelligible hybrid names like Penwortham. A second reason is the chronological span of the British names. British place-names have been dated by Jackson (1953) according to a complex series of linguistic changes which began in the fifth century and which brought about the eventual development of the Welsh, Cornish and Breton languages. The long vowel sounds found in Roose (near Barrow-in-Furness) and Preese (in the Fylde), for example, seem to belong to the period after *c.* 600. Names like Brynn could have been coined by native British speakers in the seventh or possibly even the eighth century.

The process of borrowing and assimilation is fascinating though the sociolinguistic mechanisms are ill understood. Modern theories based on studies of immigrant groups in North America (e.g. Weinreich 1963), or even on Asian families in northern England, are not necessarily applicable, but they do offer some useful guidelines. Normal social interactions including intermarriage would have contributed, but they do not explain the wholesale acculturation of British speakers. In order to understand more of the process one must consider the role of patronage in pre-Conquest society. The period covered by this chapter witnessed a transformation in the organisation of society and in the nature of kingship. No longer does one find the king as a dispenser of booty, the ring-giver of *Beowulf*. Rather he is now the source of landed wealth. The English takeover of the North-West was not motivated by the need of land for settlement so much as by the need for a new reservoir of territories and lordships which could be used for the dispensation of patronage. Lancashire was being used for the endowment of the Northumbrian church, as demonstrated by the grants of Cartmel and lands *iuxta Rippel* in the 670s, and presumably also to reward nobles and other loyal retainers.

Given these circumstances there was every incentive for native British speakers to learn English. The same was true in the colonial period in Africa and India: a knowledge of English became a vehicle for advancement under the British Empire.

The process of acculturation of the British was slow and uneven. It was most thorough along the valley of the Lune and its tributaries where British place-names are conspicuously absent. With the exception of the river name Lune, there are no known British or British-derived names, though there are several potentially early English names, including the river name Wenning and the ancient parish names of Tatham, Heysham and Melling. This was one of the most prosperous parts of the county in later Anglo-Saxon times, as demonstrated by the substantial number of pre-Norman carved stone crosses. This suggests a high level of involvement and investment in the Lune valley region. The region has a higher than average (for Lancashire) proportion of single-township and small parishes, another indication of its relative prosperity and high settlement density. Arguments were advanced in Chapter 3 for the territorial organisation of Lancashire during the fifth, sixth and seventh centuries. A case can be made out for small British kingships and/or lordships in several parts of the North-West. The Lune valley region may have formed one of these small kingdoms (a successor to the Roman period *Contrebis*?), occupying a clearly defined resource territory, extending along the Lune towards the postulated British kingdom of Craven. It would have enjoyed access to the sea and to good (by Lancashire standards) quality agricultural land along the valley bottom, and also have had access to upland grazing on the fells.

The Manchester embayment was another area brought firmly into the English orbit at a fairly early date. It is noticeable that the major river names around Manchester are all English: Mersey, Irwell, Irk, Medlock, etc. Hybrid names occur around the river crossing-points in the lower-lying parts of the embayment where the main medieval arable lay. This was a favourable settlement area, as reflected by the close packing and correspondingly small size of the townships there (Fig. 4.2). Several purely British names survived in the surrounding uplands. This suggests that Anglicisa-

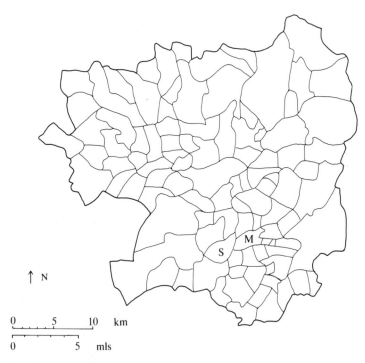

Fig. 4.2 Township size in Salford hundred

Contrast the large upland townships running in an arc from the north-west to the eastern border of the hundred with the small townships of the central and southern parts. The large townships at the south western corner encompass lowland mosses like Worsley Moss

Key M – Manchester, S – Salford

tion was a process which began at the centre and slowly, incon-
sistently, fanned outwards towards the edges of territorial units.
As identified, these territories generally occupied quite distinct
geographical regions, spreading out from the plains and valley
floors into the less accessible uplands. Some pockets of British
speakers survived in these out-of-the-way places and it is no
coincidence that **walh** (literally 'a Welshman') place-names often
lie on the periphery of identifiable territorial units. This is certainly
the case with Walton-le-Dale on the very edge of the later hundred
of Blackburn (Fig. 5.1), and with Walsden on the boundary of
Salford Hundred. Parallel situations occur in north Cheshire and
to the east of the Pennines in Yorkshire and Durham. **Walh** seems
to have been applied to native British speakers in England, being
used to denote areas where British was still being spoken when the
surrounding people were using English (Cameron 1980).

Sometimes **walh** names occur in very close proximity to known
Roman settlements, as for example Walton-le-Dale and Walton
Inferior and Superior (on the very edge of Runcorn parish in north
Cheshire) near Wilderspool. Less surprisingly, they are frequently
found in close proximity to settlements and landscape features
bearing British names, or names borrowed from the British
language, as for example Ulnes Walton in Leyland Hundred (see
Fig. 3.1). In Lancashire North of the Sands there is a Walton close
by Cartmel (granted to the community of St Cuthbert 'and all the
Britons with it'). A related name from the Scandinavian **bretar**,
meaning 'Briton', found in nearby Birkby, seems to confirm the
survival of this pocket of native British speakers into at least the
late ninth century.

Hām names and early estates

The root meaning of the element **hām** is 'a safe dwelling'. During
the early Anglo-Saxon period its sense was extended to refer to
whole villages and estates. In most place-names **hām** denotes 'a
settlement'. Its use for estate names, especially for large multi-
settlement estates, is being increasingly recognised, and it has
been claimed that, during the early decades of the Anglo-Saxon
takeover, **hām** was applied in south-east England and the Midlands
to what had been Romano-British villa estates. Villas are conspicuously absent in the North-West, and it is unlikely that villa

estates ever existed north of the Mersey. Nonetheless, it is noticeable that many north-west **hām** names lie in the same general area
as Roman military and industrial settlements. Cheetham, Kirkham,
Heysham and Penwortham lie in close proximity to the Roman
sites of Manchester, Kirkham, Lancaster and Walton-le-Dale
respectively. Unbroken continuity is highly unlikely in view of the
time-lapse of about three hundred years between the abandonment of these Roman sites and the coining of the Lancashire **hām**
names around the late seventh and early eighth centuries. Any
continuity is with lordships exploiting the same natural resource
territories and in the use of communication nodes as strategic
'central places'.

It should be remembered that other names besides **hām** were
employed as estate names. Elsewhere in the country topographical
names like Faringdon (Berkshire) were used as estate names. In
Lancashire, one, or more probably two multi-settlement groupings combined together formed hundreds in late Anglo-Saxon
times. Although there is a one in two chance of a **hām** being an
ancient parish, none has survived as a hundredal estate name in
Lancashire, though topographical names like Salford and Blackburn are found as hundred names. One should not read too much
into this, however, as decisions concerning the hundreds were
made in the tenth century and the choice depended on factors
other than continuity.

Three of the **hām** names are of special interest: they refer literally to settlements or estates held by the church. Kirkham
is 'church estate', Bispham, a name which occurs in Leyland
Hundred and in Amounderness, means 'bishop's estate'. These
names were coined from name-forming elements in currency in the
decades around 700. They are usually associated with the grant
of lands *iuxta Rippel* to Wilfrid's church at Ripon in the 670s.
It would be a mistake to identify these place-names (Kirkham,
Bispham × 2) too closely with the grants; to forget that the North-
West was already Christian territory with an established church
and clergy, even perhaps a diocesan organisation, before the 670s.
Kirkham is not necessarily the name of an entire estate or lordship
which belonged to the church at Ripon after the 670s, but arguably
a settlement on the estate based on the Fylde Ridge which already
had a (British) church. One can envisage a large estate with a
church at Kirkham, land to support the church at the Ecclestons

(more below), and a secular administrative centre at Treales. This place-name is derived from two British words, **tref** meaning 'township', and **llys** meaning 'court, hall'. In close proximity there are a number of place-names containing British elements: Inskip, Preese, and, of course, Eccleston (Fig. 4.3). The long vowel sound in Preese is a feature of the British language around 700 which suggests that native British speech persisted here for some time after the takeover. One can only speculate about the name and

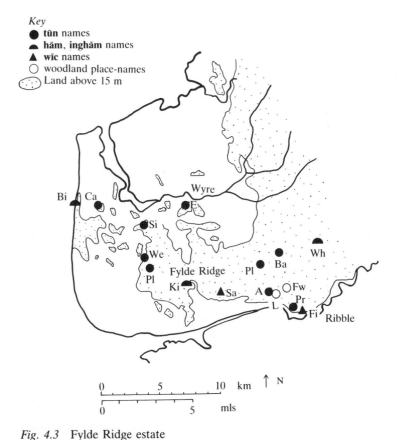

Fig. 4.3 Fylde Ridge estate

Key A – Ashton, Ca – Carleton, Ba – Barton, Bi – Bispham, E – Eccleston (Gt & Lt), Fi – Fishwick, Fw – Fulwood, L – Lea, Ki – Kirkham, Pl – Plumpton, Pr – Preston, Sa – Salwick, Si – Singleton, We – Weeton, Wh – Whittingham

extent of this multi-settlement estate. The name has not survived as a hundred name. Amounderness was borrowed from the Scandinavian name for the lordship based on the Fylde.

Amounderness encompassed the whole of the Fylde between the Ribble and the Cocker but one cannot be certain that the whole lordship was a single unity going back to the seventh century. As will be discussed in more detail in Chapters 5 and 6, Kirkham may only have occupied part of Amounderness: the Fylde Ridge and that part of the Bleasdale foothills around Whittingham which has survived as a detached upland portion of the parish. A case can be made for there having been at least two, if not three estates located in the wider Fylde Plain in Anglo-Saxon and Anglo-Scandinavian times. One of these was focused on Kirkham and Treales on the Fylde Ridge, separated from a second one, presumably centred on the Garstang area, by the River Wyre. This postulated second estate comprised an extensive amount of very low-lying land which would have been particularly vulnerable to flooding and, on balance, it is likely that its emergence was a post-seventh-century development (see Chapter 5). A third estate may have been focused on Bispham (see Chapter 6, Fig. 6.2).

The Fylde is the only area in Lancashire where one can be so certain of the survival of a British territorial lordship into the later seventh century, though one suspects they existed elsewhere, for example in the Cartmel, Wigan and Manchester areas. The survival of a number of vills owing archaic cattle renders called *Beltankou* (Beltane Cow) and *coumale* suggests that an early estate also existed at another **hām**-named site, Heysham. One or both of these renders was still owed by Overton, Heysham, Skerton, Hest, Kellet and Gressingham in the first third of the fourteenth century. With the exception of Gressingham they form a fairly compact distribution between the coast and the lower reaches of the Lune (Fig. 4.4). One explanation of this distribution is that the vills represent an early minster estate which had retained archaic forms of renders throughout the Anglo-Saxon period. Similar situations occurred elsewhere in the country where early minsters retained archaic renders, for example in the West Midlands (Hooke 1986). Gressingham probably represents a linked upland dependency of this postulated early minster estate. The name Gressingham seems to mean '**hām** where grazing took place'

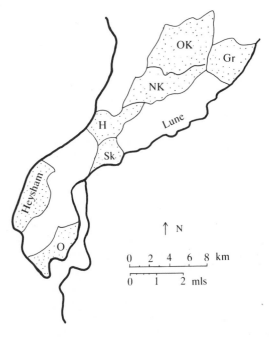

Fig. 4.4 Coumale and Beltankou renders in the Heysham area

The early estate of Heysham probably included the rest of the small peninsula between Heysham and Overton, where the townships of Middleton and Heaton with Oxcliffe lay, and Poulton (now Morecambe). These townships later belonged to Lancaster parish. Slyne with Hest and Kellet (later subdivided into Over and Nether Kellet) formed two of the three townships of Bolton-le-Sands parish, which may also have once belonged to this postulated early estate at Heysham. Gressingham came to form part of Lancaster parish as a result of an exchange.

Key Gr – Gressingham, H – Hest, NK – Nether Kellet, OK Over Kellet, O – Overton, Sk – Skerton

and the name may be a reference to a settlement used for seasonal grazing. These vills lay mostly within the larger Domesday estate of Halton in the eleventh century, but their compactness suggests that they were originally part of a smaller unit, an estate belonging to a postulated early minster at Heysham – rather than Lancaster – since the two **hām** names are likely to be roughly contemporary. The archaic renders perpetuate the Celtic system of cattle renders (see below), and suggest that the estate was an earlier British lordship transferred to the Northumbrian church around the late seventh century.

As suggested above, all of Lancashire may have been organised into a series of large multi-settlement estate groupings exploiting naturally defined resource territories. The boundaries of these estates cannot be defined precisely and so it is not possible to relate them too closely to 'central places' like Manchester. Because of this it is difficult to determine the extent to which these estates functioned as strategic territories. In the case of an estate based in the Manchester embayment an overlap is possible, even probable. The situation is less clear in the Makerfield area and in the Fylde which form obvious resource territories. Roman settlement foci existed for a time at both Kirkham and Wigan but there is no evidence to show that these locations were still acting as central places at the end of the Romano-British period, unlike at Manchester (and Lancaster and Ribchester). Yet the location of Treales so close to Kirkham, and the concentration of British place-names around Wigan suggest a continuity of some central place functions – administrative, fiscal and perhaps eclesiastical – on the part of the probable foci of these postulated British estates.

Whether one should yet call them estates, however, is perhaps debatable. Glanville Jones, who has examined the evidence for several Anglo-Saxon and medieval multi-settlement estate groupings, firmly believes that this is the case (e.g. G. R. J. Jones 1976). He suggests that the origins of estates like Aberfraw and Dinorben (in Wales) can be pushed back to pre-Roman times. The type of estate he describes, the 'multiple estate', was organised around a central *caput* manor (*maenor*), which frequently lay near a Roman site, and near a separate ecclesiastical centre. Such estates had a number of dependent settlements located for the optimum exploitation of an area's resources, arable, upland pastures, woodland, and so on. Dependent manors were tied to the principal manor which acted as a sort of fiscal clearing-house and receiving centre. Various servile dues and customs generally occurred. A pre-Saxon origin for multiple estates is disputed, however, and there is no clear consensus of opinion.

There is too little evidence concerning the internal organisation of these postulated north-western estates for one to be certain how rights of lordship were exercised. The custom of food renders probably played an important part. These renders can be divided into the three major components of the ordinary diet: bread, meat and drink. The holder of the lordship, whether king, sub-king, *præfectus* (an important official, a minister rather than a simple reeve) or bishop, would go on circuit with his household and so maintain himself (and his household) in much the same way as medieval and Tudor monarchs would on their royal progresses. Where territories were too extensive, tribute, usually cattle, was paid in lieu. The exercise of this type of lordship in the North-West need not be an Anglo-Saxon introduction. Food renders were common to both Germanic and Celtic society and could easily have continued virtually unchanged from British times. As suggested in the case of Heysham, the change lay in the beneficiary, not in the practice.

The known recipients of lands and lordships in the North-West are ecclesiastical. It is only to be expected: indeed the biographer of St Cuthbert explicitly states that the Northumbrian bishops employed *præfecti* to oversee their outlying estates. A major unresolved issue is the precise relationship between the Northumbrian church organisation and the pre-existing British ecclesiastical structure. Barrow (1973) has pointed to the correspondence between **eccles** place-names and hundreds, especially in south Lancashire. **Eccles** derives from the British *eglys, which in turn derives from the Latin word *ecclesia*. Barrow noted that there is an Eccleston place-name in Amounderness, in West Derby (the post-Conquest hundred) and in Leyland hundred. In Blackburn there is Eccleshill, and in Salford hundred, the name Eccles. He therefore drew the conclusion that these names reflected the vestiges of an early 'Mother Church' organisation whose ecclesiastical boundaries coincided with the secular administrative ones. This is an attractive theory, but one which does not quite stand up to detailed examination, for there is not an exact correlation between **eccles** place-names and pre-Domesday hundreds in Lancashire South of the Sands (Fig. 4.5). One may accept that this could be explained by administrative reorganisation after the seventh century. The hundreds are, after all, a late development Newton hundred was clearly carved out of a larger unit in the tenth century. This could easily have entailed ecclesiastical reorganisation and may be the reason why the **eccles**-named settlements did not all survive as parish centres. Eccles in Salford

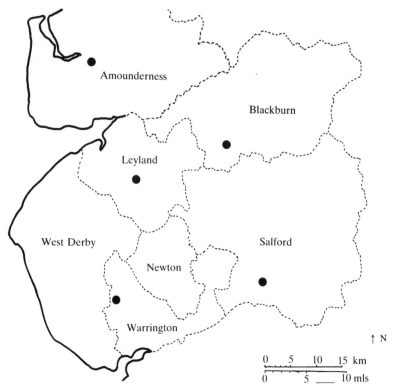

Fig. 4.5   Eccles and Domesday hundreds
Key   Place-name in *Eccles* ●

hundred did survive, as did Eccleston in Leyland. Pre-Norman sculptured stone cross fragments are known from both of these sites. It is, however, equally possible that Eccleston names should be interpreted as denoting 'the settlement belonging to the church' rather than 'the settlement where the church lay'. Clearly one must distinguish between simplex *Eccles* place-names and compound names like *Eccleston*.

The available evidence is consistent with the view that the Anglo-Saxons were taking over existing estates and lordships. There has been a rejection of the early twentieth-century picture of Anglo-Saxons coming into an empty wilderness, a thinly-settled wooded countryside where they spent centuries slowly clearing massive belts of woodland before establishing new settlements in a widespread colonisation movement. Thanks to the work of G. R. J. Jones (e.g. 1976), Sawyer (1978), Taylor (1983) and others it is now becoming increasingly obvious that not only was England densely settled in Romano-British times, but that the English countryside as a whole was being widely exploited in the seventh and eighth centuries as well. This is of course, a generalised picture; some parts of the country were relatively thinly populated and cultivated. One of these parts was the North-West and especially Lancashire. Much of the land here, as shown in Chapter 1, is marginal for settlement and cultivation. There is widespread evidence for woodland regeneration in the post-Roman centuries. This was uneven, both chronologically and geographically, but it serves to illustrate that the scale of exploitation of the landscape in Lancashire could not have been very intensive, or extensive, during the sixth, seventh and early parts of the eighth centuries.

Economic revival

From the eighth century onwards there are signs of change and reorganisation in the patterns of agriculture and settlement. Archaeologists have noticed that, with a few exceptions like Heslerton in Yorkshire, early Anglo-Saxon settlements generally took the form of small scattered farmstead groupings and hamlets. After the eighth century, population levels became more buoyant, partly in response to improvements in the climate. Settlements became more fixed, increased in size and became more like the nucleated village in appearance. This move can be linked with the higher level of social and economic stability throughout England, with the revival of the economy and the increased volume of trade. Coins began to circulate again as part of the normal process of trade. By the end of his reign, Offa had standardised the weight of the English silver penny or *sceatta* at 22 grains, a weight that was to be maintained for nearly five hundred years. In Northumbria a small brass alloy coin, the *styca*, appeared and continued in circulation until at least *c.* 867. This coin was formerly believed to have had a very brief appearance confined to the middle decades of the ninth century. New discoveries of find spots and further study have extended its chronology but there remains much work to be done before the role of the *styca* in the Northumbrian economy is properly understood. Pirie (1987) suggests that the coin first appeared in the 790s. These earliest issues have a significant silver content but after *c.* 830 they were being struck from a more coppery alloy with very little silver. It has been suggested that the use of base metal for the Northumbrian coinage was due to impoverishment in the wake of Viking raids on the North-East which began in the 790s. But it is unlikely that these raids would have been sufficiently serious on their own to necessitate the change by 830 and some other reason – an impoverished monarchy perhaps – must be sought for the apparent shortage of bullion.

Trade flourished on a local and on an international scale. Goods were exchanged at coastal *emporia* like Ipswich, *Hamwih* (Southampton), Meols on the Wirral peninsula and Whithorn. Evidence for overseas trading contacts from within Northumbria is admittedly slender but this may partly be accounted for by the requirement to re-mint foreign money. Despite this several finds of foreign coins are known in northern England, especially from York. One of the most intriguing find spots, however, is Attermire Cave (SD 842642), high up in the Ribble valley. This part of Craven lies 14 km from the boundary of the historic county of Lancashire, just to the east of Tatham. A mid-ninth-century Carolingian coin of Lothair I, minted at Dorestadt, was found at the cave, as well as one *sceat* and five *stycas*. Attermire lies far from any major settlement centre and the finds may be linked with the roughly contemporary *stycas* from the Ribblehead farmstead site, approximately 15 km further up the Ribble valley. Metcalf (1987b, p. 369) implies that the Attermire coins reached the Pennines via the Humber estuary. Yet both of these sites arguably looked westwards towards the Morecambe Bay coast, either down the Ribble, or, perhaps more likely, across to the headwaters of the Wenning and Greta and the Lune valley. A point of entry on the Irish Sea coast (Heysham for example?) is therefore as probable as the Humber.

Other examples of coins and artefacts associated with this revival of trade include a bronze shield boss and coin from Ribchester, a spearhead and *styca* hoard from Lancaster, and two *styca* hoards from the Cartmel peninsula. *Sceattas* rather than *stycas* have been found along Northumbria's south-western boundary at Manchester. In the nineteenth century a small group of *sceattas* was discovered just outside the north gate of the Roman fort (Morris 1983). A tenth-century inscribed gold ring was found nearby. Significantly this part of Manchester was formerly called Aldport, 'the old market'. These finds hint at the use of the locality as a trading venue, perhaps used on an annual basis. Free trade did not exist in pre-Conquest or medieval times and markets and fairs like Aldport and Stockport tended to develop along territorial boundaries. Chipping, which lies on the Lancashire side of what became the Lancashire–Yorkshire border, may have arisen in a similar manner. The name literally means 'a market', 'a trading place'. Its location at the upland–lowland interface may indicate an origin as a livestock fair.

The location of pre-Conquest markets and trading fairs may prove to be useful in helping to determine territorial identities in the North-West. Nor should one lose sight of the other function of markets. Just like the *vici* of Romano-British times they acted as meeting-places and places where goods as well as ideas could be exchanged. The market-places so far identified lie along the southern and eastern borders of what became Lancashire. They hint at the slowly growing economic prosperity of the North-West. Aldport can tentatively be identified with the territorial unit based on the Manchester embayment, and it probably reflects trading links with north-west Mercia. Chipping is less easy to place, though it may have acted as a trading focus for territories based on the Fylde Ridge and in the Blackburn–Whalley area.

This last-mentioned territory is surprisingly elusive in early historic times. Prehistoric activity is clearly indicated in the middle of the first millennium BC. Thereafter evidence is tenuous. Shotter (1984) has proposed a Roman base operating out of the Whalley area where a quantity of Romano-British material has been found, but its precise location is unconfirmed. A number of carved pre-Norman stone crosses have survived at Whalley and these are taken to indicate the presence of an early minster church. The identification of the Battle of *Hwælleage* of 798 with Whalley (e.g. Kirby 1965) has recently been challenged (Lewis forthcoming) and it may be that the location should be discounted on etymological grounds. It is unlikely that the area, which contains the two large Lancashire parishes of Blackburn and Whalley and which formed the eleventh-century hundred of Blackburn, had ceased entirely to have a territorial function in earlier Anglo-

Saxon times. Its strategic location along the natural east–west communication corridor along the Ribble to the Aire is too important. A few British place-names like Mellor have survived. More relevant is the place-name Wilpshire, the name of a township just to the north of the town of Blackburn. The etymology of the first part of the name presents difficulties: a British origin cannot be excluded. The second part of the name is OE **scīr**, 'shire'. This term was applied by the English in the tenth and eleventh centuries to signify the territorial unit dependent on a *burh*, and for the administrative units known as hundreds. Prior to this it seems to have been used of smaller districts and administrative units like Cravenshire, and Hallamshire, Sowerbyshire and Kirkby Malzeard (formerly Kirkbyshire) in West Yorkshire. As the map shows (Fig. 4.6), Wilpshire township today is centrally placed within Blackburn parish and may relate to a territorial unit between the Ribble and the Calder. Was Wilpshire another British estate grouping transferred into English hands and renamed?

Markets will have developed to serve communities in the northern parts of Lancashire too, but firm evidence for these is not yet forthcoming. A trading centre, perhaps a beachhead site off Heysham Head, may be postulated for the Lancaster area, especially when one considers the density of settlement there and its relative prosperity by Lancashire standards.

The basis for this wealth was still the land: sheep, cattle and animal products like hides are obviously marketable commodities. Yet whilst there is plenty of evidence for pastoral exploitation of the landscape (see Chapter 5), there is less information about the destination of the end products. Some of the wealth arising from trade and agriculture was channelled into conspicuous consumption, as represented by finds of coins and metalwork. Some wealth was diverted into land, building and various forms of patronage. It is no coincidence that monumental stonework – elaborately carved stone crosses and stone-built churches – make a reappearance in eighth- and ninth-century England. The surviving stonework of St Patrick's chapel on the headland at Heysham (Pl. 7) dates from around 900. Its 'long and short' stones and the archways forming the doorways are typical of the period. No other pre-Conquest church building in Lancashire has survived on this scale: the majority of churches were probably still built of timber. The remains of stone crosses are far more common. Edwards

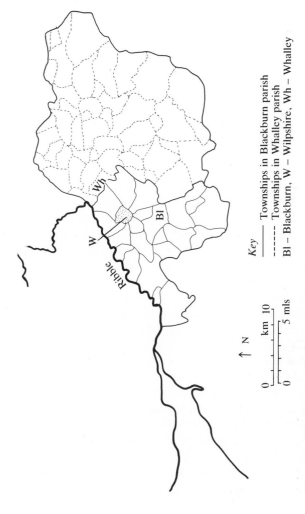

Fig. 4.6 Wilpshire in Blackburn hundred

(1978) lists around a hundred fragments which have survived into the twentieth century. Many can still be seen in local parish churches and churchyards, as at Urswick, Melling, Gressingham, Halton, Hornby, Heysham, Whalley and Winwick (Pl. 8). Some have found their way into the British Musem and the City Museum at Lancaster. These crosses are rarely *in situ*. The majority were recovered during building repair and restoration work or grave-digging. Typically the crosses are decorated with interlaced patterns or vine scroll motifs, with scenes from the life of Christ on the principal faces. They represent a considerable investment, a significant level of patronage which was sustained in many centres throughout the Anglo-Scandinavian period. Tastes were adapted to conform to prevailing cultural trends. This is particularly noticeable in the later Lancaster crosses and the churchyard cross at Halton (see Chapter 5).

The decorated crosses may well have acted as preaching crosses, being used to illustrate various aspects of the church's liturgy and calendar. The plain crosses found along the Pennine flanks fall outside this group. Examples are known from the township of Aighton, Bailey and Chaigley, from Cliviger, Godley Lane in Burnley, and Foulridge. None of these crosses was found in an obviously ecclesiastical context. The last three mentioned crosses lie within the vast parish of Whalley and may have marked the outlying parts of the ecclesiastical territory. The cross from Aighton, Bailey and Chaigley may have had a similar origin. The joint township is now included within the Yorkshire parish of Mitton, but the land where the cross formerly stood may have once belonged to Whalley. Another group of crosses which seems to have acted as territorial markers can be found in Macclesfield Forest, Cheshire. A number of fine round-shafted crosses have survived there, like that at Clulow.

These plain crosses are relatively late, apparently being tenth-or even eleventh-century in date. This was the period when the parish system as we know it began to emerge, replacing the former British and early Anglo-Saxon groupings. The minster church with its huge ecclesiastical territory, so characteristic of seventh- and eighth-century Northumbria, is poorly represented in Lancashire. The foundations at Lancaster and Whalley were probably minsters. Halton may have been a third minster site. Halton lies a few kilometres upriver from Lancaster in the Lune valley. Twelve fragments of crosses are known from there, apparently representing at least four crosses. The surviving fragments seem to belong to the tenth century and later, by which time Halton had become an important centre for control of the Lune crossings. The workshops at Lancaster and Halton overlapped chronologically and a pre-tenth-century origin for the religious foundation at Halton is highly likely.

It is not certain how Heysham fitted into this picture, and in particular its relationship with Lancaster is far from clear. Although today it is a small single-township parish, it was suggested above that Heysham was the centre of an early minster estate. It is clearly an early foundation and obviously a centre of at least local importance, boasting not only the headland chapel (succeeded by the nearby pre-Conquest church of St Peter) and the unusual rock-cut graves, but also several crosses. It is possible that Heysham was, in fact, a much earlier foundation than Lancaster, established on an Early Christian site. The 'bird's head' stone, found during the 1977–78 season of excavations there, appears to be the arm of a throne, perhaps the *cathedra* used by an eighth-or ninth-century bishop.

These crosses and sculptured stones are an outward display of the system of patronage which underpinned Anglo-Saxon society. They will have acted as symbols of a patron's power and prestige, of his ability to endow religious foundations and as a 'guarantee' of his reception in the heavenly kingdom. Such behaviour will have tended to reinforce territorial identities as secular lordships became closely associated with ecclesiastical units. The mother churches of the eleventh-century hundreds between the Ribble and the Mersey, St Mary's, Whalley (Blackburn), St Elphin's (Warrington), St Oswald's (Newton) and the others, probably date from this earlier period. **Hām**-named settlements also tended to be parish centres though none is specifically mentioned as having a church prior to the Norman Conquest. This is implied at Tatham and Kirkham, however, and Heysham had a long history as a church in pre-Conquest times. Several other settlements with early place-names, like Melling (Lune valley), may have had churches too. These churches would have been small foundations, serving a handful of settlements. Most will have been subsequently brought under the authority of a mother church. A pre-Saxon origin for some of these early churches cannot be ruled out, especially when one bears in mind the survival of names in *eccles*.

Place-names and the landscape

Lēah was commonly used for place-names in areas which were formerly woodland. The element is cognate with the Latin word **lux** meaning light, and it seems to have referred originally to sites where the woodland canopy was thin enough to allow the light through. **Lēah** names in Lancashire are thinly scattered, with the exception of the area around Leigh in the south of the county. Here there is a large grouping which includes Hindley, Shakerley, Tyldesley and Astley. This suggests that there was a belt of woodland along the hundredal boundary between Salford, Warrington and Newton. This belt forms a natural boundary between the eleventh-century hundreds, and it is logical to see this boundary as representative of an older division, going back to the time when the open countryside to the west was named Makerfield.

There are far fewer **lēah** than **tūn** (see below) place-names among the township names in Lancashire. Indeed, it is noticeable that there is a lower density of woodland place-names of any kind by comparison with, for example, Cheshire. Partly this is because large expanses of the county were covered by lowland marsh and moss where tree growth was not sustainable. Another important reason is that many of the place-names traditionally regarded as woodland indicators, names like **lēah** and **rod**, were in fact used in a quasi-habitative sense, referring to settlements established in clearings in the woodland or in a landscape that was generally quite well wooded. Much of Lancashire was settled at a relatively late date. Bowland and Rossendale, for example, were only really opened up for permanent settlement after disafforestation in the early sixteenth century. These late settlements tended to carry other names, names which are more likely to refer to the pattern of exploitation in late medieval and Tudor times. Examples include the numerous *booth* names (referring to herdsmen's booths belonging to medieval vaccaries): Barley Booth, Wheatley Booth, Roughlee Booth, Old Laund Booth, all in Pendle Forest. In fact all the townships in Newchurch chapelry (Whalley parish) were booths or vaccaries in the thirteenth and fourteenth centuries.

There were still major stands of woodland in south and east Lancashire until well after the eleventh century. Considerable expanses of *silva* (?managed woodland) were recorded by the Domesday commissioners in the south Lancashire hundreds, on Uhtred's estate in West Derby, and in Newton, Blackburn, Leyland and Salford hundreds. Domesday entries north of the Ribble are less comprehensive. Evidence for the presence of woodland there during the later Anglo-Saxon and medieval periods is provided by woodland surveys conducted on behalf of the Nature Conservation Trust and the Botanical Society of the British Isles. *Tilia cordata* (small-leaved time) is regarded as a relict species in the North-West. Fertile seed production virtually ceased after *c*. 800 BC and the principal means of regeneration are coppicing and pollarding. Stands of *Tilia cordata* are therefore believed to be indicators of ancient woodland (Piggott and Huntley 1978, 1980, 1981). The species was recorded by Piggott and Huntley in the late 1970s at Yealand Conyers and Aughton in the Lune valley, and above Ribchester along the Ribble. Despite the plantations of conifers established in recent years by the Forestry Commission, stands of ancient woodland are frequently encountered in Lancashire North of the Sands. *Tilia cordata* it quite widespread; examples are known at sites from Arnside to Coniston, and Fellows-Jensen (1985) has noted that place-names referring to woodland and aspects of woodland management predominate amongst the pre-Scandinavian names of Furness Fell. Colton seems to refer to charcoal-burners and Brantwood may mean 'burned wood'. The presence of a 'king's *tūn*' (the name became Coniston under Scandinavian influence) in the vicinity may have arisen from the need to manage the exploitation of woodland in the upland parts of Furness. The composition of ancient woodland was not, of course, exclusively lime. *Tilia cordata* was, in fact, a minority species. The principal components would have been alder, oak and birch, a pattern which goes back to pre-Roman times in the North-West.

Estate reorganisation

The most characteristic place-name element used in this period is **-tūn**, the Old English generic employed to denote a farmstead or a settlement. Gelling (1974) has demonstrated that it was used in the West Midlands to name settlements which lay in open, relatively unwooded countryside. A similar situation prevailed in the North-West. There are numerous examples in Lancashire, including Freckleton, Newton, Plumpton, Singleton in the Fylde; Urmston, Barton, Bolton, Newton in the Manchester embayment; Bolton, Crivelton and Ulverston North of the Sands. **Tūns** also occur along the main river valleys. These were all areas which had been opened up by late Roman times, areas around forts, supply bases and along the cleared zones of the Roman roads. Those areas most capable of sustaining agricultural exploitation were used and re-used for settlement. This was not necessarily an unbroken tradition of land use: some land did go out of cultivation after the main later prehistoric Romano-British clearance phase.

Large estates or lordships based on intra-related settlements are found across the whole of the country by the eighth century. In a number of cases the component settlements of these estates seem to have contributed on a socioeconomic level to the functioning of the whole. On such estates there might be bond hamlets, free hamlets, hamlets belonging to the church and king and hamlets sited specifically for the exploitation of upland and lowland resources. **Tūn**, which was already in use during the later seventh century to signify estate components as in the appellatival Kingston (literally 'king's *tūn*), is commonly found in compound place-names which appear to reflect this pattern of organisation. This is best exemplified by names like Barton, 'barley *tūn*; Chorlton, 'peasants' *tūn*; Eccleston, 'church *tūn*'; Bolton, '*tūn* of the hall'; Plumpton, 'plum-tree *tūn*'. In the Fylde there are names in Barton, Eccleston, Plumpton and Carleton (Scandinavianised form of Chorlton). In the Manchester embayment there are names in Bolton, Barton and Chorlton, as well as Eccles. This type of name will tend to predominate in regions where estates or lordships were taken over wholesale by the Anglo-Saxons. *X-tūn* place-names would have been used as a matter of convenience from the late seventh and eighth centuries onwards both to rename pre-existing British settlements and to name any new English settlements. The selection of prefix would be made according to the settlement's individual contribution to the wider economy of the territorial unit.

As these estates developed, other small settlements arose to cater for specialised needs. The element **wīc** is particularly associated with this type of small subordinate settlement. The element, which can have a range of meanings (Ekwall 1964), frequently signifies some specialised function, industrial, trading or perhaps dairying. In Cheshire it is applied to the main centres of salt production, Northwich, Middlewich and Nantwich. Its use in Lancashire place-names seems to have been less specific and it occurs with a range of specifics including words for salt (Salwick), fish (Fishwick) and barley (Borwick), and with personal names (Winwick). Names in worð, cot, and stoc, formerly taken together with wīc to denote secondary settlements of the late Saxon era, are now accepted as the smallest internal subdivisions of estates. When estates fragmented in late Saxon and post-Conquest times these small settlements became independent units, but their origin is firmly rooted in the pre-Conquest centuries.

The present writer has earlier argued the case for a correlation between these large multi-settlement estates which have socio-economic dependencies and the hundredal estates of the late eleventh century (Kenyon 1989). *X-tūn* names do tend to fall into a distribution of a single instance of a major place-name in Barton, Bolton, etc., per hundred. This is particularly well demonstrated by Salford Hundred (Fig. 4.7) where Eccles, presumably the original mother church, lies near to the main arable area around Barton. To the south lies Chorlton (later split into two townships, Chorlton-cum-Medlock and Chorlton-cum-Hardy), the main peasant settlement, a source of labour for the demesne. A ready supply of timber for fuel and building material would have been available just to the north-east around Cheetham (Brit *cęd), Cheetwood and Blackley. Ample upland grazing could be found anywhere in the arc of surrounding hills where several worð-named settlements, Wardleworth, Haworth, Blatchinworth and Whitworth, developed. Quarlton could have provided quern-stones for the estate, as the place-name is derived from the Old English word for a quernstone. The relevant names in the lordship of Amounderness have already been cited. The correlation there, however, may be with the antecedent of the dominant partner of the two or more major estates which later formed the hundred, rather than with the entire hundred.

Estate organisation in pre-Scandinavian Lancashire can therefore be described in terms of large multi-settlement estates or lordships, bound together by socioeconomic ties. These estates

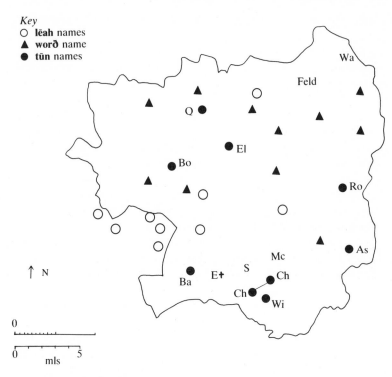

Fig. 4.7 Salford estate

Key As – Ashton-under-Lyne, Ba – Barton, Bo – Bolton, Ch – Chorlton, E – Eccles, Feld – Hundersfield, El – Elton, Mc – Manchester, Q – Quarlton, Ro – Royton, S – Salford, Wa – Walsden, Wi – Withington

were formed from British lordships transferred to English systems of patronage during the later seventh century. They were reorganised in the eighth and ninth centuries to give a level of exploitation consistent with the nature of the landscape and its agricultural potential. Good quality agricultural land was scarce and optimum exploitation was facilitated by this integration of lowland and upland resources. Groupings of large multi-settlement estates formed the basis of the late Anglo-Saxon hundreds which have tended to perpetuate their combined territories.

1 Coniston Water

2 Clitheroe Castle, © Ribble Valley Borough Council, reproduced with permission

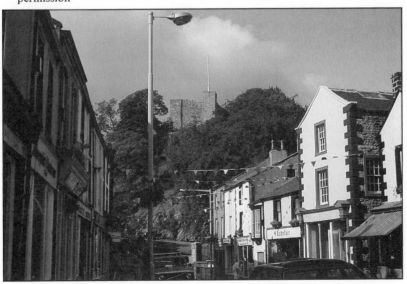

3 Rossendale, abandoned farmstead

4 Birkrigg Common and view across Sands

5 Hornby crossing of the Lune

6 Manchester *vicus*, smithing hearths

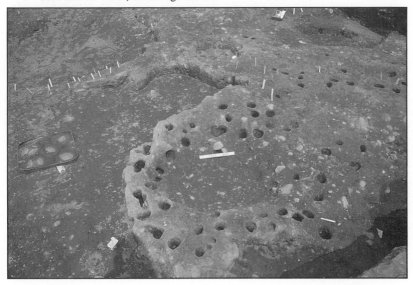

7 St Patrick's Chapel, Heysham

8 *opposite* Anglo-Saxon cross, Whalley

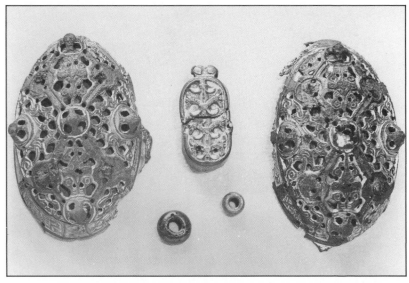

9 Claughton grave goods, © the Harris Museum and Art Gallery, Preston, reproduced with permission

10 Lancaster Castle, reproduced by courtesy of Peter Joslin

5

Anglo-Scandinavian Lancashire

Early Scandinavian involvement in the North West: hoards and *burhs*

On a national level, political events in this period are dominated by two related themes. First there is the arrival of the Scandinavians, and secondly there is the expansion of the kingdom of Wessex, which eventually swallowed up the other English kingdoms. The first recorded Viking raid on northern England was that on the monastery of Lindisfarne in 793. Thereafter raiding affected the coasts of Britain and Ireland virtually on an annual basis. By the 840s the Scandinavians were firmly entrenched in Ireland, operating out of Dublin (founded as a Viking *longphort* c. 841) and other bases. We have no information concerning Viking activity in the North-West during these years, but they must have been active in the Irish Sea area generally. The fall-off in coins from Meols, the beachhead trading site on the Wirral, between the late ninth and late tenth centuries, may hint at some initial disruption caused to coastal trade.

Raiding parties are perhaps less likely to have shown an interest in Lancashire since the region was relatively poor: its monasteries and churches were few and far between and not at all richly endowed by comparison with the North-East. Minster churches or monastic foundations seem to have existed at Lancaster and Whalley by the ninth century, and perhaps at Halton in the Lune valley. Other centres of patronage can be identified on the basis of surviving stone crosses, but with the exception of Heysham they were all on a small scale, with only one or two cross fragments surviving. The hoard of between 14 and 20 *stycas* found in the vicarage garden at Lancaster in the nineteenth century but since lost may well date from this period, as may the lost hoard of 95 *stycas* found at Lindale during the construction of the embankment to carry the Ulverston to Lancaster railway. Unconfirmed discoveries of Anglo-Saxon coins in the Liverpool area, such as those reputedly found at Otterspool on the Mersey coast, are more difficult to place. None of these hoards need be an indication of unusually unsettled times: they cannot be related to any specific threat, Viking or otherwise.

Before long the pressure increased. No longer was the danger just from ships raiding from overseas. Halfdan established his men in the area around York in 876. In the following year Mercia was partitioned. The eastern part, which came under Danish rule, was henceforth known as 'Danelaw'. After the expulsion of the Vikings from Dublin around 902 the North-West began to feel the effects in earnest. This Hiberno-Norse community was in exile between about 903 and 917. Its whereabouts during these years is unknown, though several suggestions have been offered. Some of these Vikings, like the semi-legendary Ingimundr who sailed across to Cheshire, may have attempted to establish a base along the Morecambe Bay coast. Others could have made their way across the Pennines to swell the ranks of their fellow Vikings at York. Higham has recently (1988) proposed that they established a base at the mouth of the Ribble which would have provided a safe anchorage for the Viking fleet in exile. The importance of the Ribble for the Dublin–York axis in Scandinavian times has long been recognised. This axis perpetuated the importance of the Ribble for east-west communications across the Pennines.

The Vikings did not leave Dublin empty-handed: they brought their booty with them. Some of this has turned up in the bullion and hacksilver found in the Cuerdale hoard. The hoard, which is dated to the troubled years around 905, was discovered in 1840 by workmen repairing the river embankment at the township of Cuerdale, a small place on the south bank of the Ribble just outside Preston. This stretch of the river, just upriver from the former Roman base at Walton, was one of the lowest crossing-points on the Ribble. At ordinary tides, the river is still tidal at

Walton but the tide rarely reaches as far as Cuerdale. The bulk of the collection is now in the British Museum, but some items have been retained in the North-West and can be seen at the National Museum on Merseyside (William Brown Street building).

Around 40 kg of silver was found, making Cuerdale by far the largest hoard of Viking Age silver ever found in north-west Europe. Approximately 75 per cent by weight was bullion and hacksilver, including many recognisable Irish and Hiberno-Norse brooch and ring fragments, and even a few complete rings. Of the 7,250–7,500 coins, over 5,000 coins were minted by the Scandinavian rulers of York and East Anglia, around 1,000 were English issues, and a further 1,000 were minted on the Continent (Frankish and Italian). There were also around four dozen oriental coins. Overall there is a marked Hiberno-Norse character to the hoard. This is especially noticeable in the case of the scrap silver. Only two or three recognisable Anglo-Saxon pieces have been noted, and these were likely to have been manufactured several years before the hoard was assembled. The four identified Carolingian items were also earlier pieces. It seems that the hoard was probably deposited by the Irish–Norse in exile, though the coins were largely derived from pre-existing dynasties in England and on the Continent which presumably reached the Ribble area from Yorkshire.

The hoard, then, is a mixed bag, with some older pieces, perhaps looted many years earlier on the Continent and in England, which had found their way to Ireland. The remainder had been collected recently. The York coins in particular were freshly minted issues. It may be pointed out that some of the silver and coins could have been obtained as a result of trading – rather than raiding – activities. Some of the oriental Kufic issues from Baghdad (Iraq), for example, which were minted within ten years of the deposition of the hoard, probably arrived via the Baltic routes.

The equivalent value of the hoard has been estimated at around £300,000 in modern terms (Graham-Campbell 1987), which makes it improbable that it represents the personal treasury of an individual or family. It is consistent with the pay of a war band, as has frequently been asserted in the past. More recently, however, another suggestion has been put forward: Graham-Campbell, who has made a special study of the hoard, prefers to see the

E

hoard as a political fund and links the hoard with an attempt to use the Ribble estuary as a power base from which to reassert Norse control across the Irish Sea (Graham-Campbell 1987). If this interpretation is accepted, the hoard would represent booty belonging to the exiled Irish–Norse war band, supplemented with coins and ingots from supporters from the kingdom of York or from 'Danegeld'-style payments via the York Danes.

The political situation deteriorated during the opening decades of the tenth century as the Dublin exiles re-established themselves in Ireland and also, under Rægnald, took control of the kingdom of York. The hoard from Hakirke, Little Crosby dates from this time (c. 915). It was found in 1611 when a burial ground was made for Catholic recusants. Subsequently some of the coins were melted down to make a chalice and a pix. A contemporary account of the discovery includes a drawing of some three hundred or so of the coins. (The majority were issues of Alfred and Edward the Elder, although there were a few Northumbrian Viking coins and at least three continental deniers.)

In response to the danger presented by the presence of Vikings in the North-West, and especially the threat posed by the Dublin–York axis, a number of English fortified bases or *burhs* were constructed along Mercia's north-west frontier. Ultimately the *burhs* ran from Rhuddlan and Chester along the Mersey inland to Manchester. Runcorn was the first Mersey *burh* (established before Christmas 915), followed by Thelwall, and then Manchester 'in Northumbria' before the end of 919. The location of these *burhs* underlines the strategic importance of these crossing-points for the control of movements in the North-West. The next step in the English campaign was to gain control of the Ribble estuary. First south Lancashire between the Ribble and the Mersey was annexed, arguably by Edward the Elder or perhaps by his son Athelstan. Then as the York charter dated to before 934 states, Amounderness was recovered and brought under English political control.

There is less information about the situation in north Lancashire. Around 920 Edward made a royal progress northwards. He received the submission of the king of the Scots and the rulers of Northumbria, 'both English and Danish, Norsemen and others', as well as the submission of the king of Strathclyde. In return for acknowledging Edward's overlordship and, implicitly, the supremacy of Wessex, these rulers were granted concessions. Rægnald of York was recognised as ruler of York, and a degree of legitimacy was conferred on the king of Strathclyde's tenure of lands in Cumbria annexed from ancient Northumbria. The exact extent of these lands is uncertain. The fact that in 927 Athelstan met the king of Strathclyde and the king of the Scots at Eamont Bridge suggests that the Britons of Strathclyde had taken advantage of the disruption caused by Scandinavian activity in north-west England to occupy the Eden valley. It is possible that they advanced into southern Lakeland, but unlikely that Furness and Cartmel were ever incorporated into the kingdom of Strathclyde.

Territorial reorganisation

The annexation of the land between the Ribble and the Mersey and of Amounderness involved a transfer of rights of lordship. Indeed, Fellows-Jensen has recently suggested that Amounderness was not a topographical name but an administrative one since **ness** here had the force of 'lordship' rather than headland. South Lancashire was in the hands of the prominent Mercian thegn Wulfric Spot by c. 1,000. There is no means of knowing whether his predecessors were Mercian thegns too. It is possible, if unlikely, that the lands between the Ribble and Mersey had been kept in royal hands. Certainly there was a strong Mercian association. This part of Lancashire, *Inter Ripam et Mersham* (the name is essentially a bureaucratic convenience), fell within the Mercian diocese in medieval times and was treated as an apanage of Cheshire by the Domesday commissioners in 1085–86. Amounderness, bought by Athelstan 'with no little money of my own' (presumably from the Vikings), was given to the church at York. This king of Wessex was taking great care not to alienate the leading English representatives of Northumbria whose appointment he himself confirmed. There was a strong tradition of separatism in the North and Northumbrian magnates, lay and ecclesiastical, were as eager to ally themselves with Scandinavian rulers as with southern English kings. It would have been politically insensitive to transfer its control, ecclesiastical and political, into southern hands. Athelstan went out of his way to pay reverence to the Northumbrian saint, St Cuthbert, endowing his shrine with precious offerings. Thus Amounderness was restored to the diocese of York, and placed in the hands of the church. It is possible that in doing so Athelstan was actually restoring the lordship to ecclesiastical hands. As seen in the previous chapter, the lands *iuxta Rippel* granted to the church of Ripon in the 670s probably formed part of this area.

It is also interesting to note that Athelstan apparently purchased Amounderness from the Scandinavians. The 'reconquest' of England was not just carried out on the battlefield, but involved considerable negotiation and bargaining. A few years earlier two other estates were similarly transferred for money. One lay in Bedfordshire, the other was an estate in Derbyshire. Athelstan's charters confirming the title of these estates observe that both had been purchased on the instructions of Edward the Elder and Æthelred of Mercia. The nature of these transactions underlines an important aspect of the Scandinavian involvement in the North-West. The Scandinavians in the early decades of the tenth century were not necessarily motivated by land hunger in the generally understood sense. They were not all looking for land on which to settle and raise crops and flocks. As later in the century, many were opportunists, looking to raise a capital sum to finance ventures elsewhere.

The transfer of these lordships in the tenth century emphasises the fact that Lancashire still did not exist as a single territorial unit. Instead one finds large multi-centre estates grouped together to form larger units, the lordships identified as Amounderness and the lands between the Ribble and the Mersey. Between the level of estate and tenth-century lordship another layer of territorial organisation can be discerned. This is the hundred. The hundreds, the internal subdivisions of the shire, became formalised administrative units throughout much of England during the late ninth and tenth centuries. In south Lancashire, six hundreds had come into existence by Domesday, each treated as hundredal estates with their own *caput* manor. Amounderness was not, strictly speaking, recognised as a hundred until after the Conquest, though it is generally regarded as one. Lonsdale is a post-Conquest development.

Prior to the Anglo-Saxon period, loosely-defined resource territories have been identified in the North-West. These can often be associated with the control of strategic communication nodes. The Manchester embayment is a good example. These territories were subdivided into smaller units of exploitation, the multi-settlement estates of the eighth and ninth centuries, based on places like the Fylde Ridge, Manchester embayment and the Makerfield area. Crossing-places were still significant for general purposes of communication, and especially for the siting of markets. But control of them was less vital for the economic success of an estate, and there is no reason to suppose that estate centres were situated with this aim in mind. This state of affairs changed in the tenth century. Attention was again focused on control of strategic communication nodes.

Higham has suggested that after the annexation of south Lancashire, Edward the Elder intended to create a new advance *burh* at Penwortham (Higham 1988). This would have been used to defend the Ribble estuary and prevent its use as a Scandinavian base. Penwortham is an ideal choice for this. It is on a low spur projecting out into the Ribble which was subsequently the site of a Norman motte-and-bailey castle. Excavators working on the motte in 1856 found an 'organic layer' deep into the mound, and suggested that it represented earlier activity on the site. Unfortunately the associated finds could not be closely dated and this attribution, however plausible, cannot be confirmed. Penwortham lies right on the northern edge of Leyland hundred, across the river from Preston in Amounderness, and slightly downriver from the former Roman site of Walton-le-Dale. Walton lies on the extreme western edge of Blackburn hundred and the hundred boundary actually snakes around here to include it. Walton is one of only five named Domesday vills in the entire hundred of Blackburn and so obviously a measure of importance was attached to its location which gave access to the major north-south crossing-point of the lower Ribble (Fig. 5.1).

Preston, across the river, is the third place positioned to take advantage of this crossing-point. The name Preston literally means 'settlement of the priests' and Ekwall (1922) interpreted this as meaning that Preston was an old rectory manor. Alternative suggestions are possible. Higham, for example, suggests that its name was given after 930, perhaps in recognition of a church established here by the archbishop of York, the new lord of Amounderness. It is noticeable that the parish lies sandwiched between the two parts of Kirkham parish. It looks as if it could have been carved out of an older, more extensive unit, such as

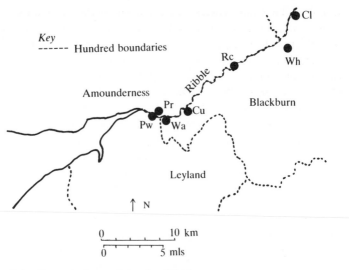

Fig. 5.1 Central places along the Ribble

These central places were strategically located at crossing-points. Note the way that the boundaries of the three hundreds meet at the lowest crossing point of the Ribble

Key Cl – Clitheroe, Cu – Cuerdale, Pr – Preston, Pw – Penwortham, Rc – Ribchester, Wa – Walton-le-Dale, Wh – Whalley

the eighth-ninth century estate based on the Fylde Ridge. By the eleventh century Preston was recognised as the *caput* manor of Tosti's estate of Amounderness. This shift of emphasis from the Ridge to the Ribble surely belongs to the years around 930 and reflects the importance of access to, and control of this stretch of the river.

Warrington provides another example of a shift in the focus of an estate or lordship from the agricultural heartland to a peripheral crossing-point controlling access to a territory. Runcorn guarded the lowest tidal crossing of the Mersey and Warrington lay at what was the lowest non-tidal crossing of the river in ancient times, as commemorated in the minor name Latchford. This crossing was recognised by the Romans when they established their industrial base just across the river at Wilderspool in the first century. Edward the Elder placed a *burh* along the same stretch of river, at Thelwall. These sites are both on the Mercian side of the river. Once the territory to the north had been brought firmly into the English orbit, it would have made sense to move across the river, thereby gaining the political advantage of a base in what had been Northumbria. As Warrington began to function as a *de facto burh*, there would have been a need for some internal reorganisation in the hinterland of Warrington. This provides a likely context for the creation of the hundred based on Warrington, a strategic territory; and perhaps for the emergence of a new administrative unit, the aptly named hundred of Newton. As Figure 4.5 shows, the hundreds of Newton and Warrington have obviously been carved out of a larger territorial grouping, the suggested 'Makerfield'. The original focus of Makerfield lay to the north, presumably in the Wigan area, where there is a concentration of British place-names, some names coined as late as the eighth century. The remnants of the lordship were presumably grouped together to form the small hundred administered from Newton. Newton, it may be noted, lies strategically along the line of the Roman road northwards from the Mersey crossing to the Ribble crossing. Once military attention became focused on the Mersey crossing, however, the importance of the Makerfield area dwindled and it was overshadowed by Warrington.

Further support for the importance of Warrington comes from the archaeological evidence. The presence of a fortified site at Warrington underneath the medieval castle at Mote Hill is suggested by Kendrick's excavations of the nineteenth century (Kendrick 1852–53). Two Anglo-Scandinavian jet gaming pieces, now in Warrington Museum, confirm that there was activity at the site above the level of peasant farmers. A large number of log-boats have been found along the Warrington stretch of the Mersey, and fragments of at least eleven boats are known. A further two have been found at Barton and Irlam (Irwell). Nine of these boats have been radiocarbon dated. Without exception the boats belong to the years around AD 1,000 and McGrail argues for a probable 'in use' date in the eleventh century (1979). The boats have certain common features suggesting a characteristic technique for log-boat building in the Mersey area. Log-boats were probably used for ferrying, fishing and fowling, and for the collection of reeds. Hypothetical reconstructions made of one of the Warrington boats (Warrington 2) indicate that it was capable of a good speed and that it could have operated as a 'bulk' cargo-carrier or personnel carrier.

The Manchester embayment was also affected by military and political considerations in the tenth century, and in particular by the decision to station a garrison at Manchester in 919. This move reinforced the 'central place' functioning of the locality and its use as a strategic territory. Opinion is divided about whether the *burh* was a refurbishment of the Roman fort or a new construction at the other end of Deansgate where the core of the medieval town lay. A pre-Norman date for the so-called 'Angel-Stone' in the cathedral has been rejected (Coatsworth 1983), however, and the distribution of finds from the Anglo-Saxon period also favours the Castlefield (i.e. fort) area. The eleventh-century hundred is not named after Manchester but takes its name from Salford. This is a topographical name of a type favoured by the earlier Anglo-Saxons to designate large, multi-settlement, territorial groupings. The *caput* manor of the eleventh-century hundredal estate presumably lay somewhere in the vicinity of the present town of Salford, not in Manchester, and it seems likely that the *burh* was extremely short-lived. Salford was a royal demesne manor in 1066 and reverted to crown hands for a time in the post-Conquest period, before eventually becoming part of the honour of Lancaster. Its development in post-Conquest times was quite separate from that of Manchester (see Chapter 6), though how far back this duality can be pushed is far from certain.

At least one large multi-settlement estate exploited the Manchester embayment and the surrounding uplands in the eighth and ninth centuries. Others will have developed by the eleventh century as the tenurial arrangements became more fragmented. It is striking that Salford township lay within the large medieval parish of Manchester (Fig. 5.2). One might logically have expected it to fall within the parish of Eccles along with the other townships to the west of the Irwell which belonged to the medieval manor of Salford. One possible explanation for this is that Eccles was formerly a much larger ecclesiastical unit, encompassing the medieval parishes of both Eccles and Manchester. In support of this one may point to Eccles's early name, its circular churchyard, and the surviving sections of pre-Norman carved crosses. Consequent upon the foundation of the *burh* at Manchester a separate ecclesiastical parish was created. This in itself does not explain

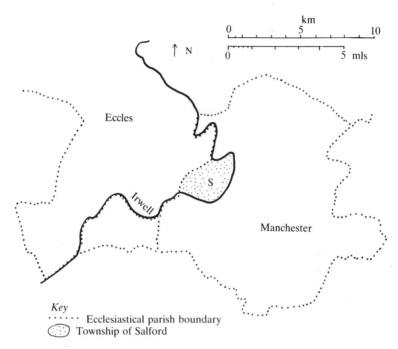

Fig. 5.2 Salford and the ecclesiastical parishes of Eccles and Manchester

why Salford was included within Manchester parish, but one can only suppose that its inclusion was a deliberate policy, perhaps designed to retain an earlier secular administrative centre located at Salford. This centre seems to have maintained a measure of independence from Manchester during the tenth century and, once immediate strategic needs were satisfied, it (re-) emerged as the *caput* of the eleventh-century hundred. A similar pattern of ecclesiastical reorganisation attendant upon the creation of a *burh* has also been noted at Runcorn in Cheshire (Higham 1988).

It is noticeable that events of the tenth century lead to a repetition of the Roman pattern of occupation of strategic crossing-points along the Ribble, Mersey and Irwell. There is less information for the situation to the north of Amounderness but it is reasonable to suppose that a similar pattern prevailed there in response to the general threat posed by Scandinavians in the North-West. There is no firm evidence for any military activity in the Lancaster area, no suggestion of an early *burh* or similar foundation. The production of carved stone crosses continued, seemingly unaffected apart from the appearance of new stylistic influences. Scandinavian motifs are clearly discernible in products from the Lancaster and Lune valley workshops after the late ninth century. Some of these works have close affinities with tenth-century Anglo-Norse crosses from the Isle of Man, as exemplified by the Hart and Hound stone from Lancaster (Fig. 5.3), and with an interlace-decorated fragment from Melling in the Lune valley.

The sculptured stones highlight a major problem for the interpretation of archaeological remains. How is an artefact to be interpreted when it displays features from two different cultural traditions? Is it an English object produced under Scandinavian

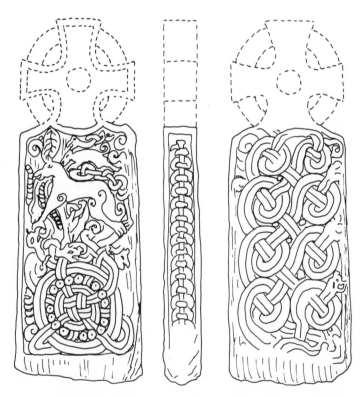

Fig. 5.3   Lancaster 'Hart and Hound' stone (after Collingwood 1927)

influence? Is it a Scandinavian object with English influences? Or is it a product of a truly hybrid, and integrated culture? Was it made by native-born English craftsmen adapting to new fashions? Was the patron a person of English or Scandinavian origin; did it even matter to him? Was he pagan, Christian, or a new convert with ambivalent beliefs about the afterlife? On the whole it seems safer to see such artefacts as a product of the mixed cultural climate of the tenth and eleventh centuries in England as a whole, not just the North-West, rather than a statement of a man's ethnic background and political allegiances. Similar *caveats* may be expressed about small portable items like the Manchester roundel. This tenth-century piece of ornamental metalwork is clearly a product of the southern Danelaw, but its presence at Manchester indicates no more than a general level of contact with the Danelaw. This could be a trading contact, and need not imply the presence of any Danish settlers in the Manchester area.

The same applies to the cross which still stands in the churchyard at Halton in the Lune valley. This large cross is decorated with relief carvings illustrating, on one side, scenes from the life of Christ, and on the other, scenes from the pagan heroic Sigurd legend. Cramp (1979) has assigned the cross to her Phase VII, *c.* 890–954. This phase of pre-Norman sculpture is characterised by the active combination of Scandinavian ornament with traditional Anglo-Saxon styles. Bailey has argued that there was a monastic centre at Halton which produced this and other cross fragments known from Halton. Associated cross fragments can be seen at Gressingham church. The location of an important sculptural workshop reflects Halton's position as a centre of patronage and secular lordship in the tenth century. The Halton hoard of silver coins deposited around 1025, together with a plaited torc, in a silver-gilt bowl of Continental manufacture may represent the personal treasury of the holder of this lordship in the first part of the eleventh century. The hoard was found during the enclosure of Halton Common in 1815 and subsequently dispersed, some going to local people, the rest to London. The hoard contained 860 silver pennies and what seem to have been six gold coins. (Less than half the coins have been listed, and apart from the twenty-one deniers from Normandy, most were issues from the reign of Cnut, produced at the York mint.)

This lower Lune valley lordship can be associated with Tosti's

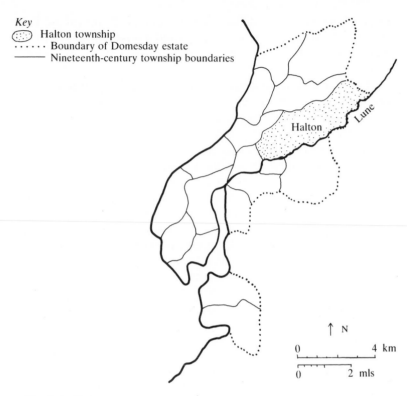

Key
- Halton township
- ····· Boundary of Domesday estate
- ——— Nineteenth-century township boundaries

Fig. 5.4 Halton estate

six-carucate estate of 1065, though, of course, it may not have covered exactly the same area. In the middle decades of the eleventh century the estate whose *caput* lay at Halton extended down to the estuary of the Lune, including Lancaster and Heysham and land on either side of the mouth of the Lune (Fig. 5.4). It is debatable whether the Halton estate would have included Lancaster in the tenth century. Possession of Lancaster would, however, have given control of the estuary as well as of the lowest non-tidal crossings of the Lune. If Lancaster did not belong to Halton, then who held it? As noted above, production of crosses continued without any discernible break. But if Lancaster was in English hands, why was a base not established there to control movements in and out of the estuary, as happened at

Penwortham–Preston on the Ribble and at Runcorn on the Mersey? Could the Lune have harboured a Viking fleet after the Ribble and Mersey had been closed to Scandinavian ships after c. 930?

These large territorial estates and hundred groupings in Lancashire South of the Sands developed in response to the events of the tenth century. The Scandinavian invasions provided the opportunity for the kings of Wessex to impose their supremacy, swallow up Mercia and absorb much of the former kingdom of Northumbria during the course of the century. The northern boundaries of eleventh-century England, ruled from a power base in the South, now ran through what had once been the kingdom of Northumbria. In the North-West the boundaries were probably quite fluid. The status of north Lancashire, Cumberland and Westmorland (the modern Cumbria) is uncertain. The area was variously claimed by kings of England, Strathclyde and Scotland. By the second quarter of the tenth century much of the area we know as Cumbria was regarded as part of Strathclyde. In 945 Edmund wrested it from Dunmail of Strathclyde and bestowed it on Malcolm of Scotland. Thereafter it seems that the Duddon was regarded as the boundary between the kingdoms. One cannot tell for certain whether Furness and Cartmel had formed part of the lands held by Dunmail, but the fact that this area does not seem to have formed part of the grant to Scotland suggests that it had remained in English (or Anglo-Scandinavian) hands. Whatever the case, by the eleventh century Furness and Cartmel were firmly within the English orbit. This is shown clearly by Fig. 6.4 showing the holdings of the Northumbrian earl, Earl Tosti, in the North-West. The Lune valley watershed was a recognised part of English Northumbria and Tosti's large multi-settlement estate based on *Hougun* encompassed most of Furness (Fig. 6.3). The small number of manors across the Duddon near Millom are insufficient to establish any definite pre-eleventh-century contact with Copeland.

Scandinavian settlement

It is not know exactly when the first Scandinavians set foot on the shores of Morecambe Bay. The expulsion of the Vikings from Dublin around 902 and the construction of *burhs* along the Mersey over the next seventeen years provides one context, but one cannot rule out an earlier presence. The redemption of Amounder-ness by around 930 gives another date. Sometime in the first third of the tenth century much of Lancashire seems to have been under Scandinavian control. But what exactly did that signify? It was enough to bring about a renaming of the Fylde region which henceforth was known as 'Agmundr's lordship', a Scandinavian name perpetuating the Scandinavian genitive/possessive inflexion in -ar. It caused a renaming of the hundred based on Merseyside, Derby, later West Derby, to distinguish it from the county town of the East Midlands, and arguably gave the name Furness to the Scandinavian lordship established in Lancashire North of the Sands. But was there a mass settlement of Scandinavians? Or was there a selective take over of key settlements and estate centres?

Archaeological evidence is of little use because it is so thin on the ground. There are two dubious Scandinavian burials reported from Rampside and Heysham, where a hog-back stone survives. Another hog-back is known from Bolton-le-Sands. These stones are regarded as Scandinavian grave-markers and have a specific distribution in northern England in areas of Scandinavian settle-ment (Lang 1984). It is possible that some of the doubtful Anglo-Saxon burials, like that from Inskip, could be Scandinavian. The radiocarbon date for the Quernmore find would just allow for this to be an early pagan Scandinavian burial. The only certain example is the burial from Claughton on the edge of the Fylde Plain found in 1822 when workmen were busy constructing an access road to the hall. They disturbed a Bronze Age tumulus, uncovering not only a primary prehistoric burial, but also the remains of a Viking Age burial. Several weapons (since lost) were found, as well as a pair of 'tortoise' brooches fastened together to form a small casket. These brooches are typical of the first half of the tenth century and hundreds have been found across northern Europe from Iceland to Kiev. More interestingly, however, is the third 'brooch'. This small decorated silver-gilt and niello oval is in fact a converted Carolingian baldric mount. Carolingian material, as exemplified by the grave goods from Balladoole (Isle of Man), is rare in Viking Age graves in Britain, though, as noted above, a small amount was found in the Cuerdale hoard. The Claughton mount was not of recent manufacture and may have been looted on the Continent in the late ninth century, i.e. around the same time as the Cuerdale pieces. This would suggest an early, rather than mid-century date for the Claughton burial.

On the whole, though, the archaeological evidence for pagan Scandinavians is slender. One reason for this may be that the Scandinavians, although pagan at this period, did in fact bury their dead in Christian cemeteries. This certainly seems to have been the case at Heysham and Rampside, and at Ormside in Westmorland. The only certain example of a pagan burial does not, it is true, come from a Christian context, but it does reflect the tradition of re-use of former burial sites.

Archaeological evidence for settlement sites is even less forthcoming in the North-West and archaeologists are coming to recognise the difficulty in distinguishing between English and Scandinavian dwellings, farmsteads and other domestic sites. Ribblehead, which lies just outside the Lancashire border on the western flank of the Ingleborough massif, about 2 km from the Roman road connecting Lancaster and Bainbridge, highlights the difficulty in assigning an ethnic origin to an archaeological site. Three rectangular stone buildings have been excavated and a number of small plots and fields lie outside the enclosure. Occupation during, or soon after the third quarter of the ninth century is attested by the associated Northumbrian *stycas*. The coins are indisputably English and there is nothing necessarily Scandinavian about either the finds or the buildings. Yet many archaeologists argue that this is a sheiling site, Scandinavian in origin, which relates to the river valleys and lowlands west of the Pennines (King 1976). In support of this one may cite the numerous examples of Scandinavian sheiling place-names (e.g. those in **erg**) on the limestone fells of eastern Cumbria and the central Pennines.

Place-names

Place-name evidence helps to fill out the sparse archaeological record (Fig. 5.5). As with earlier British and English names, the use of Scandinavian names is not without problems. Old English and Scandinavian are cognate languages; they belong to the same group of languages and share many common features of vocabulary, grammar and syntax. A number of words are virtually the same in both languages. One also has to recognise that a number

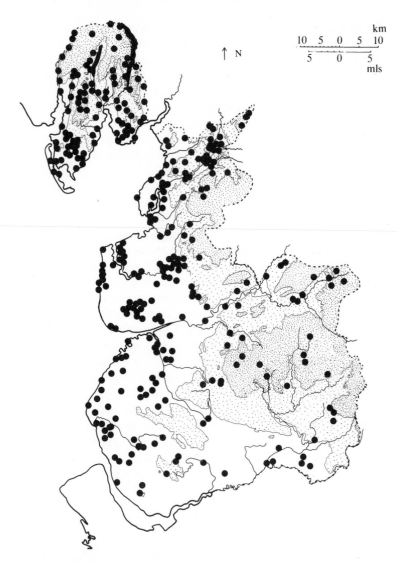

Fig. 5.5 Scandinavian place-names in Lancashire (after Fellows-Jensen 1985, Ekwall 1922 and Wainwright *et al.*, unpublished collection of field names in the Lancashire Record Office)

The map shows the distribution of recorded names containing Scandinavian elements. It is not a map of Scandinavian settlement (see text) of Scandinavian words were borrowed into the local dialect, and so although of Scandinavian origin, their use for place-names, including field names, is not in itself direct proof of Scandinavian settlement. This is especially true of minor names and field names in Carr (ON **kjarr**, 'alder vegetation'), Holme(ON **holmr**, 'water meadow') and Thwaite (Scand **þveit**, 'a clearing'). The last mentioned, **þveit**, has survived independently in North Country dialect with the sense of 'forest clearing', 'land reclaimed from forest or waste'. Smith (1956) argues that the term was in current use during the Middle English period as the name for new clearings, and this was obviously the case in the central Eden valley – Inglewood area.

The use of personal names as indicators of ethnic origin is fraught with difficulties. Fashions in naming come and go and, as seen today, personal names are more likely to reflect an individual's social class and aspirations than his or her cultural or ethnic background. One can readily envisage a situation in eleventh-century England when it was a positive advantage to bear a Scandinavian personal name like Cnut, especially if one aspired to move among higher circles. Place-names traditionally accepted as indicators of Danish settlement in the Greater Manchester area, names like Flixton and Turton, are just as likely to have been named for Englishmen called Flikkr and Thuri.

The work of place-name scholars like Cameron (1965, 1970, 1971) and Fellows-Jensen (1972, 1978a, 1985) has introduced another 'grey area' for settlement studies. They have argued convincingly that a significant number of Scandinavian place-names were given to pre-existing English settlements; a village bearing a Scandinavian name was not necessarily founded by – or even lived in by – Scandinavians. Names that fall into this category include Kir(k)by names of which there are a number of examples in the North-West, including one on Merseyside, a second in Furness, and the Domesday name of Cartmel. These are clearly all settlements associated with a pre-existing church. Other possible examples are names like Rawcliffe on the River Wyre, which is a literal translation into Scandinavian of the name Radcliffe, 'the red cliff'. The Domesday form of this place-name was *Rodeclif* but Scandinavian forms like *Routheclive* and *–routheclif* predominate during the following centuries.

The latest research into the location of settlements whose names have Scandinavianised forms or which seem to have been renamed shows that, in the majority of cases, the settlements will tend to be favourably located with regard to soil fertility, drainage, water supply, and so on. This is generally true for Scandinavian names in Yorkshire, the East Midlands and the whole of the North-West. One must be careful, however, not to assume that all Scandinavian-named settlements must have been renamed if they are favourably situated, whilst those lying on poorer locations are genuine Scandinavian foundations in areas formerly unoccupied by the English. Environmental factors may be vitally important in determining settlement viability in the North-West but they are not the only factors involved.

It is easy to be negative about the extent of Scandinavian naming in Lancashire. The above mentioned caveats must be observed, but even if all the place-names about which there is a shadow of doubt are rejected, this still leaves a significant body of undisputable Scandinavian names (Fellows-Jensen 1985). These include habitative names like Scales, Arkholme, Sowerby and *Swainset* (now Swainshead), and purely topographical names like Wray, Larbrick, Norbreck and Kellet. Scandinavian topographical names are more common in the North-West than habitative ones, in contrast to the situation in the Midlands. This reflects the overall toponymic pattern in Lancashire. Population levels were generally low, and consequently settlements were sparsely scattered across the landscape. The need was, therefore, for topographical points of reference rather than habitation names.

Exactly how many settlers are represented by this body of Scandinavian place-names? Again one can adopt either a 'minimalist' or a 'maximalist' point of view. Sawyer (1971) has argued for a relatively small-scale Scandinavian settlement; place-name scholars favour a more extensive immigration. The question hinges on how many people are needed to effect a linguistic shift. Opinions vary considerably on this issue, but it has been argued that a very small number of politically or socially dominant people could bring about a change in the spoken language. This certainly seems to have happened during the fifth to seventh centuries, during which time the British language and British place-names disappeared over much of England. On the local level, the Scandinavians seem to have been politically dominant for only a short space of time in the North-West, for decades rather than for centuries.

There are a large volume of Scandinavian minor names and names which occur as the 'junior partner' in joint townships where the senior partner has a British or English name. This is particularly noticeable in the Fylde where the following occur: Inskip (British) with Sowerby, Preesall (British-OE hybrid) with Hackinsall, Layton (OE) with Warbreck and Little Eccleston (British-OE hybrid) with Larbrick.

The survival of these names probably owes more to the date of their coining than to any mass Scandinavian immigration. Throughout the country place-names were becoming more fixed as written records began to proliferate. Once names were entered on to fiscal listings, etc., they acquired a permanence lacking in earlier centuries. In North Wales, in places like Anglesey, for example, there are numerous Scandinavian names, yet this area was certainly not densely settled. It may be that the hundreds of minor names in Lancashire were coined by a minority of Scandinavian speakers over a lengthy period of time.

The longevity of the Scandinavian language in the North-West can be questioned. Some scholars have accepted the runic inscription from Pennington (North of the Sands) which records Gamel's building of the church there in the twelfth century, and the thirteenth-century runic inscription from Conishead Priory as evidence of a continued Scandinavian linguistic tradition. Page, who has examined the epigraphic evidence (Page 1971), suggests that there was a re-introduction of the Scandinavian language from the Isle of Man. This suggestion fits in with Fellows-Jensen's theory (1983) concerning the origin of Scandinavian place-names in the North-West. Traditionally it has always been accepted that the main thrust of the settlement came from across the Irish Sea (Wainwright 1945–46). Norse Vikings, who had spent some time in Ireland and were perhaps joined by some Irish adventurers, crossed the Irish Sea to establish new settlements along the western coasts and plains of Lancashire and in the Wirral. Settlers from the east of the Pennines are credited with a small-scale penetration into north-east Cheshire and south-east Lancashire, largely on the basis of the distribution of Hulme place-names and the presence there of place-names like Flixton containing supposedly typical Danish personal names.

The problems in using personal names have already been mentioned and the use of test words like the East Scand **hulm** and the

West Scand **holmr** to distinguish between areas of predominantly Danish or Norwegian settlement has now largely been discounted. The variation between Hulme and Holme names reflect Anglo-Norman scribal practices and local dialects as much as any ethnic Scandinavian difference. Indeed, the Hulme names in the Greater Manchester area could be post-Conquest formations dating to the time when the element had been borrowed into the English language. There is less controversy over the group of place-names associated with the Irish contribution. This is seen in names like Ireby in the Lune valley and Ireleth in Furness. Both derive from the ON word **Írar**, 'Irishmen'. Other place-names contain Irish words or personal names. The Irish connection is indisputable, but questions arise about the scale of their contribution. As seen above, there is a good historical and archaeological context for the arrival of Hiberno-Norse settlers coming across from Ireland after 902. But, as Fellows-Jensen has pointed out (1983, 1985), there are very few similarities between Scandinavian place-name types in Ireland and north-west England. Place-names in **bȳ**, for example, are virtually non-existent in Ireland though common in the Danelaw. A few of the Scandinavians may have crossed over the Pennines to Lancashire from the Danelaw and York via the Ribble–Aire Gap. This may explain names like Westby and Ribby on the Fylde Ridge. But many of the closest parallels for Lancashire names are found in the Isle of Man where names like Sowerby, Nateby and Derby (Jurby) occur. There are also affinities between sculptural styles and decorative motifs between the two areas. The interlace on the Melling cross fragment and on the Hart and Hound cross from Lancaster have close parallels in the Isle of Man. Fellows-Jensen believes that the Isle of Man Scandinavians came from the Danelaw via Strathclyde. If this interpretation of the names is correct, and it is certainly consistent with the available evidence, then this means that there were originally two distinct groups of Scandinavians in the North-West.

The likely progression of the Scandinavian settlement as reconstructed from archaeology, place-names and documentary sources begins with an initial settlement via Ireland which was short-lived and which involved largely opportunists and adventurers, the 'true' Vikings of legends. This occurred during the first third of the tenth century and saw the takeover from above of large English estates. It was accompanied by a wave of renaming and

Fig. 5.6 Scandinavian place-names in south-west Lancashire and Uhtred's Domesday estate

ended with the political reconquest of Lancashire by Edward and Athelstan. This was followed by a sporadic, possibly small-scale and certainly protracted immigration via the Isle of Man over a hundred years or so which has left no documentary record but which is responsible for the proliferation of minor names.

When one looks at the distribution and nature of Scandinavian names locality by locality the sequence of settlement can be followed and details of the political organisation and economy can be reconstructed. In south-west Lancashire, for example (Fig. 5.6), the distribution of Scandinavian place-names can be contrasted with the distribution of English ones. There are only a few Scandinavian names in the Liverpool area, that is, the area south of the River Alt. They are names like Roby, Kirby, Crosby, West Derby and Formby. They represent a small Scandinavian enclave delimited by Roby, which literally means 'boundary settlement'. These Scandinavians had their meeting-place at Thingwall. The enclave is virtually surrounded by English-named settlements like Everton, Childwall, Woolton, Huyton and *Wibaldeslei*. Some, if not all of these Scandinavian names probably represent renamed English sites, with perhaps some 'infill' settlement. Certainly names like Kirby and Kirkdale are likely to indicate pre-Scandinavian settlements associated with a church. Crosby, 'settlement with the cross', is another candidate for renaming. Formby, too, may be such a settlement for the name may mean 'the old settlement'; perhaps this had been an abandoned English settlement. The situation on this part of Merseyside can be compared with that across the Mersey in Wirral. There too is an assembly site, Thingwall, and a boundary settlement, Raby. The townships in this part of the Wirral are appreciably smaller in size than those to the south and east of the peninsula, reflecting the 'packing' of settlement. In both areas, important multi-settlement estates were apparently held by loyal English subjects to neutralise the political power of the Scandinavians settled there. Uhtred's Domesday holding surely represents the English bulwark on Merseyside. It included English-named settlements and some Scandinavian-named ones, including Roby, Kirkby, Crosby and Skelmersdale. Ormskirk, although not mentioned specifically by the Domesday Survey, was contained within the limits of Uhtred's estate.

The inclusion within this estate of Scandinavian-named settlements suggests that by the end of the tenth century progress had been made in recovering control over English settlements which had previously been in Scandinavian hands. In marked contrast, across to the north of the Alt, there is a string of Scandinavian names along the coastal dune and moss belt, and along the fringes of Downholland Moss – names like Hesketh, Ainsdale, Birkdale, and the lost names *Otegrimele*, Argarmeols and Ravensmeols. The last two belonged to settlements washed away by subsequent coastal erosion. Settlements in this part of south-west Lancashire seem to represent a freer pattern of settlement, a true external colonisation of open spaces in the landscape. It is noticeable that, before the availability of modern drainage techniques and fertilisers, this was amongst the poorest, most marginal land in the county. The topographical nature of these names must be heeded. However, there is no reason to suppose that the settlements which later bore these names were necessarily established by Scandinavian settlers. They could just as easily be late Saxon or even post-Conquest in origin.

A similar mixing of Scandinavian 'colonisation' of the mossland fringes and apparent renaming of existing English settlements occurs in the Fylde (Fig. 5.7). On the ridge itself Kirkham shows unmistakable Scandinavian influence in the surviving name forms. Just off the main part of the ridge, Carleton is the Scandinavianised form of Chorlton. Places like Ribby and Westby, however, are so ideally located to exploit good quality land that it is hard to see them as new settlements in the tenth century. Geographical determinism has been set aside for the south and east of England, but cannot be dismissed so readily in the North-West. Well-drained land on the Fylde Ridge was at a premium in an area where so much of the land was susceptible to flooding from the river Wyre and its tributaries, or was poor quality peaty soil. The better drained sites would have tended to attract early settlement. Small settlements like Larbrick, Norbreck and Warbreck, on the other hand, all of whose names refer to a cliff or slope of some kind, may well be peripheral colonisations. They indicate an interest in these marginal soils, suggesting some level of exploitation, if not settlement, in Anglo-Scandinavian times.

The overall distribution of Scandinavian names in the Fylde may throw light on the organisation of estates there. The concentration of Scandinavian place-names, both topographical and habitative names, along the low-lying land flanking the Wyre is

Fig. 5.7 Major Scandinavian place-names in the Fylde

striking. They run from Hackinsall at the mouth of the Wyre, past
Rawcliffe and Catterall, to Garstang and beyond up into the
Wyresdale uplands. This part of Amounderness to the north of
the Wyre was split between three parishes in post-Conquest times,
but most fell within either St Michael's or Garstang parish. St
Michael's claimed seniority over Garstang church in the early
thirteenth century but the jury which sat to investigate the claim
found that St Helen's Garstang had never been a chapel attached
to St Michael's; it had always been regarded as a mother church
(Farrer 1902: 197). How long, one may ask, was 'always' in the

minds of thirteenth-century jurors? There are good reasons for thinking that St Helen's was one of the three churches mentioned in Amounderness in 1086. Garstang was one of the most highly assessed vills in the lordship of Preston, being rated at six carucates, the same of the *caput* manor. 'Always' surely stretched back from the reign of John to that of his great-great-grandfather, the first Norman king. Moreover, Garstang seems to have acted as the meeting-place for the Scandinavian community in the Fylde. This is obviously not a *Thing* name but it is a name characteristic of a meeting-place. Garstang means 'a pole with a gore or blemish' and may denote a pole that was sufficiently distinctive to act as an assembly marker. Nearby there is the place-name Kirkland, which is in fact the name of the ancient parish of Garstang. The name derives from the Scandinavian **lúndr**, not **land** as might be expected. **Lúndr** has an especial significance since it is a term used not just for 'a wood', but it also can have the sense of 'a sacred grove', which might indicate a focus of pagan worship under Scandinavian lords in the early tenth century.

All things considered, there is good reason to attach a measure of importance to Garstang. The Viking Age burial at Claughton lay within the parish which is also suggestive. If not the eponymous Agmundr, this may yet have been an early tenth-century Scandinavian lord of the Garstang area. The later fitz Reinfrid lordship of Garstang may represent a revival of this earlier tradition of lordship, which geographically and strategically was situated centrally on the main north-south communication corridor running between the Ribble and Lune crossings along the edge of the Fylde Plain.

The density of Scandinavian place-names around Garstang can be contrasted with the scarcity of Scandinavian place-names further south in the area around Preston. The townships in Preston parish bear English names, reinforcing the impression that Preston was an administrative and political centre for the 'reconquest' of Amounderness after Athelstan's redemption of the lordship.

Settlement expansion and the sheiling economy

A large proportion of Scandinavian place-names refer to sheilings. These include names in **erg** (a Scandinavian loan from Gaelic **airghe**), **skáli** and **sǽtr**, like Anglezarke, Scales and Hawkshead.

Many of these sheilings, especially those with **erg** names, lie at fairly low altitudes, below 200 m, and were probably used as spring and autumn pastures rather than pastures grazed in the height of summer (M. C. Higham 1978). These sheilings must have been linked with lowland settlements but it is rarely possible to demonstrate these links formally. Goosnargh, part of the detached upland portion of Kirkham parish, is one example. Ortner in Wyresdale, literally 'Overton's **erg**', has been identified as the **erg** belonging to Overton, a small township near the Lune estuary. Hawkshead was obviously used as upland pasture by the people of Low Furness. The use of upland pastures, although characteristic of the Scandinavians in their homelands, is by no means peculiar to Scandinavian farmers in the North-West, and there is no reason to suppose that the Scandinavians introduced a fundamental change in the basic pattern of exploitation of the landscape. Transhumance is a most efficient way of raising livestock and the practice probably dates from pre-Roman times. Similar patterns of linked settlements forming early multi-settlement estates have been described elsewhere in the country. Indeed, Della Hooke's study of the West Midlands charters suggests that linkage was the norm rather than the exception (e.g. Hooke 1986). Certainly the link between the pastures of the Goosnargh area and Kirkham was already well established in the pre-Scandinavian period. This is illustrated by the early **inghām** name of Goosnargh's adjacent township, Whittingham, also a detached part of Kirkham parish. In Leyland Hundred links between upland and lowland townships have been revealed by Mary Atkin's study of stock tracks (Atkin 1983). Characteristic enclosures and tracks ruuning between Croston parish and its detached upland dependency Chorley can be traced on the Tithe Maps. Further north, the inhabitants of Bolton-le-Sands claimed the right to drive their beasts over Lindeth Marsh to Yealand Conyers. When they were resisted in 1530 a riot broke out (VCH VIII: 164).

Areas of early upland pastures may be denoted by **feld** names. **Feld**, from the same common Germanic root as Dutch **veld**, can mean 'treeless heath' and seems to have been used by the early Anglo-Saxons to designate areas above about 300 m which were used for common grazing by communities based in the lowland plains and valley floors. There are a number of pre-Conquest **feld** names running along the Pennines from Cantsfield to Hundersfield

(Rochdale parish), Dukinfield and Macclesfield. On the east of Pennines similar names include Huddersfield, Wakefield and Sheffield.

One question that is difficult to answer is whether there has been any renaming of sheiling sites, or whether the Scandinavian sheiling names reflect an extension of the practice. This in turn raises the whole issue of settlement expansion in the later Anglo-Saxon period. It is generally accepted that this was a time of rising population levels, a time when the climate was warming up and facilitating the extension of settlement, especially at the upper margins. The resurgence of cereal pollen levels and of other indicators of open land is marked in (unpublished) pollen diagrams from Anglezarke and Rivington Moors and from the lowland mosses at Pilling and Cockerham (Oldfield and Statham 1965). Scandinavian names belonging to this phase are relatively easy to identify, and it is tempting to assign the Scandinavians a leading role in the movement of external colonisation which saw the extension of settlement along the edges of mosses and moors and up into the Pennine valleys. But, as argued above, none of these names, whether Scandinavian sheiling or topographical name, need indicate permanent settlements occupied in the pre-Conquest era. On balance it is preferable to see them as evidence of seasonal occupation at best. They will not have developed into permanent settlements until the medieval period. The spread of **worð**-named settlements in Rossendale Forest falls into the same category. These run from Longworth and Edgeworth near Bolton, through Wardleworth near Rochdale, and on to Butterworth on the Yorkshire border. Typically these **worð**-named townships lie on high ground, above 152 m, on thin acid soils which are prone to erosion, and probably represent seasonally occupied enclosures associated with livestock farming.

Given the low level of rural productivity in Lancashire it is perhaps not surprising that there is so little evidence for any great opening-up of the landscape in later Anglo-Saxon times. the degree of exploitation of the landscape may not have been all that different from that of the eighth century, despite all the evidence for an opening-up of the economy nationally. Names formerly associated with secondary colonisation, **cot**, **stoc** and **wīc**, are now better seen as indications of the fragmentation of pre-existing estate units. This could have arisen under the pressure of incoming

Scandinavians, but is perhaps more likely to be because of the virtually universal increase in population levels since there is an increasing likelihood of fission of estates between children at times of population growth. **Lēah**, once regarded as an indicator of woodland clearances in the later Anglo-Saxon period, is now treated as a contemporary with **tūn**, and does not necessarily indicate an expansion of settlement after the ninth century. There are a few instances where clearances are a possibility, however. One example is on the edge of the Fylde Plain where pollen diagrams from Cockerham and Pilling mosses (Oldfield and Statham 1965) suggest a renewal of activity in the later Anglo-Saxon period. There are two **lēah** names here, Cleveley and Winmarleigh. Another example is the lower slopes of Rossendale around Mossley and Stalybridge in the parish of Ashton-under-Lyne. Both of these instances suggest the beginnings of the external colonisation which became so prevalent after the Conquest in the North-West.

6

Parish, barony and shire: the emergence of Lancashire

There was still no political unity to the area which became the historic county of Lancashire at the opening of the eleventh century. The north-western counties of Cumberland and Westmorland did not formally exist then, either. This part of the North-West was still organised around a series of large multi-settlement estates. In Great Domesday Book, the southern hundreds are appended to Cheshire as lands 'Between the Ribble and Mersey'; Amounderness and the other lands to the north are found with the Yorkshire folios since they formed a north-western region of lordship dependent on York. The Ribble was to continue as the dividing line for some time yet to come. The boundary zone along the Ribble is even reflected in local dialectal forms of the pre- and post-Conquest period. The Mercian pronunciation of certain vowel and consonant sounds is found in place name forms as far north as the Ribble but rarely beyond. Mercian **wælla, wælle** rather than Northumbrian **wella** is found in Childwall; the Mercian palatalised *c* in **æcer** survives as a soft 'g' in Cliviger. The Middle English dialectal zones are less well defined. Nonetheless there is a general trend for North Country forms to predominate in the northern half of the county (perhaps under Scandinavian influence), whilst Midland forms occur to the south of the Ribble. Old English **ce(a)ster** therefore becomes *caster* in Lancaster, yet survives as *chester* in Manchester and Ribchester. The boundary between *a* and *o* forms in certain place-names also runs along the Ribble, *a* forms predominating to the north.

The major source for this period is, of course, the Domesday
Survey, compiled after twenty years of Norman rule (Morgan
1978). It is by no means a complete gazetteer of settlement,
especially south of the Ribble where there are so many unnamed
settlements or 'berewicks'. Nonetheless it is the most comprehensive listing of Lancashire manors, or more properly of administrative and fiscal units, before the Great Inquest into knight's fees of
1212 (Farrer 1903). A number of early Lancashire charters have
survived as well which can be used to supplement the two surveys.
Many of these documents were edited by Farrer at the turn of the
century (e.g. Farrer 1902, 1903 and VCH) and his work, though
not without error, forms the basis for modern studies.

Landholding on the eve of the Conquest

In many ways Great Domesday Book is a retrospective document,
looking back at territorial dispositions and revenues at the time of
King Edward as much as under William. Even so there are errors,
for Earl Tosti was recorded as having still been in possession of
Amounderness and estates in north Lancashire in 1066 when
in fact he had been driven out of his earldom of Northumbria
in autumn 1065. He was replaced by Morcar, brother of Earl
Edwin of Mercia. Morcar's tenure seems to have been ignored
by Domesday commissioners in the North-West, though not in
Yorkshire to the east of the Pennines. This suggests that Morcar
had not had time to visit the North-West and claim the remainder
of his estates.

Domesday Book shows that in Lancashire as a whole by the
eleventh century, there was a preponderance of large multi-
settlement estate groupings whose origins go back to the pre-
Scandinavian period, but whose foci are likely to have been
relocated to cater for the changed requirements for defence during
Scandinavian times. To the south of the Ribble these had been
held as royal demesne estates, perhaps since Cnut's execution of
Wulfric Spot's heirs earlier in the century; to the north of the
Ribble they were held by the Northumbrian earl. There were also
a number of smaller estate units, especially in the northern part of
the county. Sometimes only one or two settlements are named
within these estates in Great Domesday Book, occasionally more.
What they all have in common is that they were relatively small,

and were held neither by King Edward nor by earl Tosti. Ulf, for example, held nine carucates in Melling, Hornby and Wennington in the Lune Valley; Orm held eight carucates in Holker and Birkby; Duuan held six carucates in Cartmel (*Cherchebi*); Ulf (? the same Ulf) and Machel had two carucates in Lonsdale and Cockerham. Ulf and Orm were fairly common personal names of the period and, while these two tenants probably did hold other lands in the North, it is difficult to be certain.

In the past, efforts have been made to correlate each of the Domesday hundreds with individual multiple estates dating back to earlier centuries (e.g. Barrow 1973; Higham 1979; Kenyon 1989). There is certainly a loose tradition of exploitation of the territories which had developed into hundreds by the late eleventh century. These relate to geographically-rooted resource territories and the control of communication nodes over which specific lordship rights seem to have developed. During the Anglo-Saxon period, clearly defined estates developed within these lordships, in the Fylde, in the Manchester embayment, around the confluence of the Ribble and Calder, in Furness and Cartmel. Somehow, during the course of the tenth and eleventh centuries, some of these estates were welded together to form Amounderness and the south Lancashire hundreds recorded in Great Domesday.

An impression of the pre-eleventh-century estates can be obtained through a study of the ecclesiastical parish structure. In the North-West, parishes tend to be large multi-township units, frequently with detached portions representing former patterns of exploitation of the landscape. Some, especially the very small parishes, must postdate the Conquest, but the larger ones like Blackburn, Whalley and Kirkham have earlier origins. These large parishes are closely defined by natural boundaries, by rivers and other landscape features. It is widely accepted that these were broadly conterminous with secular estates at the time when tithes became firmly established during the tenth century.

Blackburn is a particularly good example of a hundred made up of two large compact parish blocks (Fig. 4.6). The forty-five townships of the vast parish of Whalley together with twenty-four townships of the parish of Blackburn form the hundred. The creation of the diocese of Blackburn is a modern development. Whalley is essentially an upland parish whose landed focus lies at the confluence of the Ribble and Calder. Blackburn, which lies in the western part of the hundred, has its share of upland but also has a greater proportion of valley-bottom land along the flood plains of the lower reaches of the Ribble as far as the former tidal limit at Walton-le-Dale. Blackburn parish can be associated with the postulated early secular unit of Wilpshire. Together these two parishes encompass a territory which commands the western end of the Ribble–Aire communication corridor, a strategic territory which can be traced back ultimately to the first millennium BC hillforts of Portfield and Castercliffe.

Newton is another two-parish hundred. It roughly corresponds with the parishes of Winwick and Wigan. This hundred, often called Makerfield, seems to represent the core of a much earlier lordship, one which arguably had a British origin. Both Winwick and Wigan have circular churchyards, though only Winwick, which incidentally possesses the remains of an extraordinarily large pre-Norman sculptured cross-head, is specifically mentioned in Domesday.

Elsewhere in south Lancashire tenurial fragmentation has distorted the earlier parish structure. The degree of tenurial fragmentation in West Derby hundred has frequently been commented upon (Higham 1979). Unnamed berewicks or dependencies are the rule in Great Domesday Book's entries for south Lancashire. Unnamed thegns held a total of 109 unnamed berewicks in the other five hundreds. In West Derby hundred, however, there are only six unnamed berewicks, the dependencies of the royal manor; elsewhere individual settlements are named, together with most of their tenants at the time of King Edward. Assuming the name to refer to a single individual, Uhtred held 17 vills plus half of Marton. Thirteen others are named as tenants of around 30 named vills. Besides these, there are a further 11 vills held as 39 holdings by 2 priests and a number of thanes and *radmen* (comparatively free tenants owing riding duties; Farrer 1898). This intensive fragmentation is generally attributed to the impact of the Scandinavians on settlement and estate organisation, and indeed to the land market generally in tenth and eleventh-century England. Land was now being bought, sold and exchanged as people sought ways of raising money to pay the various fiscal dues and gelds.

Walton-on-the-Hill was apparently the mother church of the hundred though a priest is also listed under Childwall, which was presumably a dependency by the eleventh century. Both have circular churchyards and a pre-Norman cross is known from Walton. Another early parish lay to the north of the hundred at Ormskirk. This is not listed in Great Domesday but the place-name implies the existence of an earlier church which would have served Uhtred's estate. Significantly, the church has a circular churchyard and a fragment of a probably pre-Norman cross.

The parish situation in Salford hundred has already been discussed. It is particularly complex, reflecting the intensity of settle-

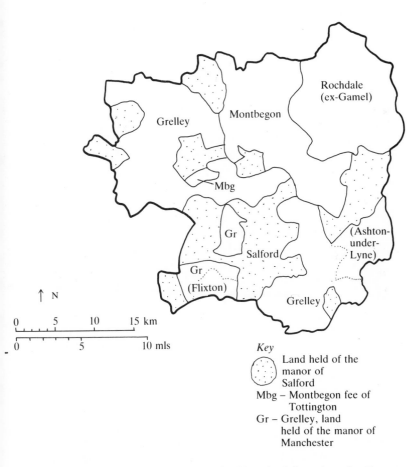

Fig. 6.1 Post-Conquest estates in Salford hundred (based on the Great Inquest of 1212)

F

ment and the high level of sub-infeudation in post-Conquest times (Figs. 6.1, 6.7) which has distorted earlier linkages. Great Domesday Book refers to two churches which held land in Manchester, St Mary's and St Michael's. These are usually associated with the parish churches of Manchester and Ashton-under-Lyne, though a good case can be made out for St Mary's Eccles having been the mother church of the hundred. Rochdale is another candidate for a pre-eleventh-century ecclesiastical unit. Gamel's two-carucate holding formed a discrete territorial unit tucked away in the north-east corner of the hundred. The antiquity of the estate is corroborated by the name by which it was known in the eleventh century, *Recedham*, a potentially early **hām** place-name. Rochdale did not always lie happily within the Manchester embayment lordships; in 1212 Hugh de Elland held Rochdale of the de Lacy honour of Clitheroe.

Great Domesday is far less informative about the settlements of the Northumbrian earls lying north of the Ribble (Farrer 1900). In the case of Amounderness, it is stated that Tosti held Preston and that a further fifty-nine settlements, of which only sixteen have 'a few inhabitants', belong there. The list includes many of the modern townships, as well as a few settlements which have since either been lost or have shrunk in importance, such as *Aschebi*, a lost vill in Myerscough, or *Swainset*, now known as Swainshead, in Wyresdale. Crimbles, Threlfall and Newsham are amongst those which have since lost their independent status. Amounderness was not strictly speaking a hundred and several possible estates can still be identified (Fig. 6.2). Preston, which arguably replaced Kirkham (and Treales) as the focus for the Fylde Ridge estate, was not the only sizeable manor in Amounderness. At six carucates it was equalled by Garstang, Ribby, Layton, Staining, Thornton, Singleton and Preesall, and exceeded by Bispham which had eight carucates. Even allowing for the possibility that Preston had a favourable tax rating, the local importance of places like Garstang, which developed into a market town, and Bispham should not be overlooked.

A case has already been made for the existence of a Scandinavian estate to the north of the Wyre focused on Garstang. Bispham is another interesting possibility. Its name has been linked with the seventh-century estate granted to the church at Ripon, and even though Bispham remained a chapelry attached to Poulton parish

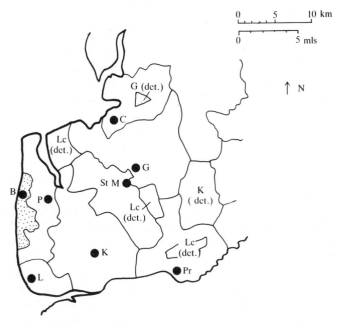

Key
⬭ Bispham Chapelry

Fig. 6.2 Fylde parishes

Bispham has been carved out of Poulton parish. Kirkham had a large detached portion encompassing the townships of Whittingham and Goosnargh. The several detached portions of Lancaster parish reflect forest holdings

Key B – Bispham, C – Cockerham, G – Garstang, K – Kirkham, L – Lytham, P – Poulton, Pr – Preston, St M – St Michael's, G (det.) – detached portion of Garstang parish, K (det.) – detached portion of Kirkham parish, Lc (det.) – detached portion of Lancaster parish

until the seventeenth century, the church has early antecedents. There was already a chapel there by 1147 when Bispham was the subject of a dispute between the abbeys of Shrewsbury and Séez (in Normandy). The source of this dispute can be traced back to the 1090s when Lancaster Priory and Shrewsbury Abbey were founded by Roger of Poitou and his father, Roger of Montgomery, respectively. Lancaster was founded as a daughter house of Séez. The first two abbots of Shrewsbury also came from Séez, prompting Farrer's suggestion (1902: 283) that it too had been intended as a daughter house of Séez. As shown by the ensuing disputes over Bispham and Kirkham, there was some confusion about which lands had been given to Shrewsbury and which to Lancaster. That Bispham and Kirkham were both apparently given as endowments by Roger of Poitou raises the possibility that Bispham formerly enjoyed a higher status. The lands involved a teamland in Bispham, together with the tithes of Layton and Warbreck. Today Bispham, Layton and Warbreck form the parish of Bispham. It has developed around the chapel, presumably founded by monks from Shrewsbury to oversee their interests in this detached portion of their endowment before the estate was granted to Lancaster Priory in exchange for other lands. Bispham is surrounded by the parish of Poulton-le-Fylde (Fig. 6.2), and arguably the two together once formed a multi-settlement estate whose secular focus lay at Bispham and which extended along the Fylde coast from the mouth of the Wyre to the mouth of the Ribble. It is not possible to determine whether the single-township parish of Lytham, which formed the endowment of a small Benedictine cell of Durham Priory founded between 1189 and 1199, originally belonged to this unit or to Kirkham parish. Nor can one be certain how far back this postulated estate can be traced. It is presumably later than the seventh-century British lordship based on the Fylde Ridge, but one cannot say whether it is earlier than the establishment of the lordship of Amounderness, by 930.

Great Domesday notes that there were three churches which belonged to Preston. There may have been others which escaped mention because they were considered to be dependent chapels rather than mother churches. *Michelescherche* is listed as a Domesday vill and although the presence of a church is implied, it is far from certain that this was one of the three churches. Garstang and Poulton (including Bispham) are surely two of these churches; Kirkham (first documented in 1094) is likely to have been the third. Arguably, then, these three parishes represent three secular pre-Conquest units which had been brought together under the lordship of Amounderness. Each of these postulated estates was based around a compact lowland grouping of settlements. They would have been linked to upland pastures (and woodland?). The link between that part of Kirkham parish which lay along the Fylde Ridge and its detached upland portion of Whittingham and Goosnargh has already been discussed (Chapter 5). Garstang parish was well placed to exploit the Bowland fringes from Claughton to Wyresdale. The third postulated estate lay along the coast, apparently cut off from direct overland access to the hills. Access could have been managed by stock tracks allowing movement of livestock through other territorial units by agreement and custom, of the kind proposed by Mary Atkin (1983).

The lands north of Amounderness had not been subjected to the same degree of administrative reorganisation and regrouping into hundreds, or wapentakes as they are sometimes called (the term has a Scandinavian origin), as has the land between the Ribble and the Mersey. Lonsdale hundred is an entirely post-Conquest creation which gave an administrative unity to the miscellaneous estates which lay to the north of Amounderness. Two large, multi-settlement, pre-Conquest estates organised around a *caput* manor can be identified, Halton and Furness. The compact estate of Halton extended from Halton itself downriver to Lancaster, and included a stretch of coast from Overton, Heysham and Poulton-le-Sands (later known as Morecambe) right up to Bolton-le-Sands and Carnforth (Fig. 5.4). This estate guarded the approaches of the Lune and the lowest crossing-places over the river. Again the core of the estate lay in the lowlands but there was a tradition of linkages with upland pastures. As noted in the previous chapter, the men of Overton apparently had rights of seasonal grazing in what became Wyresdale Forest. The men of Lancaster similarly claimed rights in the Forest of Quernmore.

In Lancashire North of the Sands there was a similar large estate grouping which by 1086 was focused on *Hougun* and which encompassed the Furness peninsula (Fig. 6.3). The identity of this *caput* manor is open to question. The place-name is the dative plural from of the Scandinavian **haugr**, 'a mound'. Earlier authorities have followed Farrer (1900) and taken it to be an earlier, lost name for Millom, which lies, not in Furness, but across the River Duddon in Copeland. Yet as long ago as 1922 Ekwall proposed Haume, a place near Dalton in Furness, which certainly makes more sense both geographically and etymologically. Winchester (1987) has followed this alternative and it is the *caput*

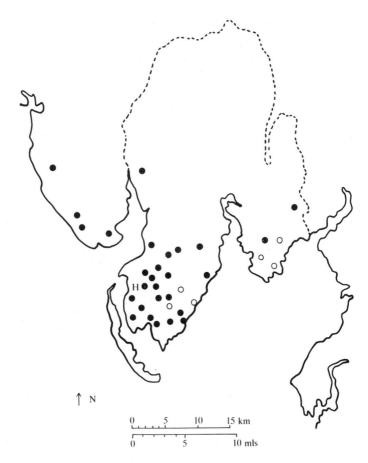

Key
● Manors named in Great Domesday Book as belonging to *Hougun*
○ Other Domesday manors
H – possible site of *Hougun*

Fig. 6.3 Tosti's Domesday estate of *Hougun*

manor recognised here. This large estate was able to exploit a wide range of resources: sea and shell fish along the coast, lowland arable in Plain Furness, and upland grazing on Furness Fell.

Earl Tosti held both of these estates in 1065, as well as a third, smaller, multi-settlement estate based on Whittington. Whittington comprised land in the far north-east of the historic county and extended into what later became parts of Yorkshire and Westmorland. By the twelfth century this estate had lost its integrity: only three Domesday vills survived in the then newly recognised county of Lancashire: Whittington itself, Thirnby and Newton. Together they formed the medieval parish of Whittington.

The break-up of Tosti's Whittington estate highlights the major problem for understanding the evolution of Lancashire's northern boundary. The Lune watershed marks a geographical boundary zone loosely observed by eleventh-century estates, but the boundary of the historic county of Lancashire owes more to dispositions and feudal lordships of the twelfth century than to earlier ones (Fig. 6.4).

Key
- - - - - Boundary of the historic county
———— Domesday estates (after Morgan 1978)
------ Possible Domesday estate

Fig. 6.4 Domesday estates and the county boundary in north Lancashire

The internal organisation of eleventh-century estates

Details concerning the internal organisation of these estates are only forthcoming in the case of the south Lancashire hundredal estates. There is no information about the internal organisation of the estates north of the Ribble. It is unlikely that the pattern of exploitation would have been significantly different but, as they were not crown demesne, it is debatable whether services and customs would have been as rigorously enforced.

South of the Ribble a fairly uniform series of customs and dues were enforced, though there were a few concessionary exemptions. It is highly unlikely that these renders have survived intact from British times, or even from the eighth and ninth centuries. It is noticeable that renders in kind (part of the *feorm* or 'provender rent'), which are a characteristic of other royal manors like Cirencester, are not found in south Lancashire in the eleventh century. Renders in kind, which would have formed the basis of the fiscal economy of an estate organised into economic dependencies, would be most practical in a relatively thinly settled landscape. By the tenth and eleventh centuries, a standardised system of rents and dues would have been easier to collect. It is possible that these had been imposed after the annexation of south Lancashire (by *c.* 930), but a more likely context is the tenth to early eleventh century, when Athelstan and then Cnut managed to acquire the lands between the Ribble and the Mersey, the latter after the death of Wulfric Spot and his heirs. The *Beltankou* and/or *coumale* renders which were owed by a handful of vills in north Lancashire can, it was argued in Chapter 4, be seen as a relic of much earlier British tribute payments.

The customary rents and dues exacted from the pre-Conquest royal estates *Inter Ripam et Mersham* are set out at the end of the West Derby entry; they include payments of 2 ora of pence for each carucate, work on the king's buildings, fisheries, woodland enclosures and stagbeats, as well as a day's harvesting in August 'to cut the king's corn'. Fines for assault, rape, theft, highway robbery, breaking and entering and a breach of the King's peace are prescribed, as are fines for failure to attend the Shire Moot, or to perform service. Fines were also payable if one wished to leave the king's land or to inherit one's father's land. The exact dues varied slightly from hundred to hundred. In Newton, for instance, the men of the hundred reaped for two extra days in August; the men of Leyland and Salford did not owe work on the king's hall, nor did they perform reaping services. A handful of thegns had exemption from some of the customary dues. These included Uhtred and Dot in West Derby, and Gamel in Salford Hundred. Two free men of Newton had exemptions from certain customs and had 'the fines for bloodshed and violence to women, and the pasturage of their men'. These exemptions probably originated as incentives and rewards given to loyal thanes. Church holdings were also generally exempt. St Oswald's 'of the village' (Winwick) and St Mary's, Whalley, for example, held two carucates of land exempt from all payments, while St Elphin's (Warrington) held one carucate exempt from all customary dues except tax. The churches of St Mary and St Michael in Salford Hundred held one carucate of land in Manchester with a similar exemption. These concessions no doubt arose out of considerations of piety.

Hundredal organisation in south Lancashire

By the eleventh century all of England south of the Tees had been shired. Each shire was based on a *burh*, and it acted as a major functional unit in the prevailing system of local government. The shire was subdivided into smaller units, the hundreds, to facilitate the collection of taxes and the administration of law and order. There has been much debate about the origin of the shire organisation and it is generally agreed that the first recognisable shires appeared under Alfred in late tenth-century Wessex. The system was extended into the West Midlands, probably under Edward the Elder. Shires did not always respect earlier territorial units in western Mercia. Shrewsbury, for example, became the focus of a shire formed by an amalgamation of two Anglo-Saxon tribal groupings, the *Wreocensæte* and the *Magonsæte*. The shire based on Chester made its first appearance during the tenth century, being first documented in 980. The circumstances surrounding the annexation of south Lancashire to Mercia have already been discussed and it is clear that by 1086 south Lancashire was being treated as an apanage of Cheshire. The precise administrative status of the lands Between the Ribble and the Mersey is not known. A hundredal organisation clearly existed in south Lancashire and several other features of the late Anglo-Saxon shire are also found. The Domesday listing of customs specifically refers to the office of Reeve (*præpositus*) and to the duty of attendance at the Shire Moot (*siremot*). This suggests that certain elements of the shire administration had been introduced in south Lancashire. The shire assembly referred to may have been the one for Cheshire; but in view of the special position of these six hundreds as royal demesne it is safer to assume that they had their own assembly. Although south Lancashire had a quasi-shire organisation, this did not extend to north Lancashire. There was no comparable hundredal organisation and Lancashire did not fully develop a county structure until the reign of Henry II.

The development of the county of Lancashire

The creation of the historic county can be considered on two levels. Firstly there are the political events which lead to the granting of estates in north-west England to Roger of Poitou after the Conquest. His possession of lands both North and South of the Sands and of the Ribble paved the way for the unification of territorial lordships focused on Lancaster. Secondly, there is the detailed consideration of the feudal holdings which comprised the ancient county and which determined its precise boundaries.

Roger of Poitou, the third son of the Conqueror's cousin Roger of Montgomery, was entrusted with estates in the North-West after the northern rebellion and subsequent 'Harrying of the North' of 1070–71 which left behind a trail of waste vills in the North-East, in Cheshire, and, perhaps, in the Fylde. The laconic Domesday statement about the fifty-nine vills dependent on Preston, '16 of them have a few inhabitants . . . The rest are waste', is usually taken to be a reference to the damage, though it could have been caused when Tosti was ousted in 1065. William believed that Roger was sufficiently strong – and loyal – to guarantee the behaviour of the population.

Roger's tenure of Lancashire was not without its problems. The Domesday Survey tells us that Roger had held (*tenuit*) the land between the Ribble and the Mersey; that he had enfeoffed a number of men-at-arms there; and that 'now the king holds' (*Modo tenet Rex*) these six hundreds. In other words, some time before 1086 Roger had lost control of this area. Similarly, in Amounderness we are told that Roger of Poitou 'had them' (*habuit*), but presumably has them no longer. The changing fortunes of Roger of Poitou in Lancashire have been the source of much discussion, revolving around exactly what he held, and when he held it. Originally he seems to have been granted control over the former royal hundredal estates in south Lancashire. Then, in 1071, after the rebellion of Morcar and Edwin, Roger of Poitou was granted Amounderness and perhaps Halton. This gave Roger effective command of a huge territory in the north of England. As well as the estates which later comprised most of Lancashire South of the Sands, he had extensive holdings in the Craven district of Yorkshire, including the multi-settlement estate based on Grindleton. Some time between 1071 and 1086 Roger then lost these Lancashire estates – either because of rebellion or as part of a land-exchange deal. He subsequently regained his Lancashire estates under William Rufus and was also given Furness and Cartmel. In the early 1090s, therefore, Roger of Poitou was lord of the area which became known as Lancashire South of the Sands and Lancashire North of the Sands. Roger was to hold on to these estates for about a decade before they were finally confiscated in 1102 after he joined his brothers in another rebellion, this time against Henry I, the Conqueror's youngest son. The grant of this extra territory in north Lancashire to Roger is to be seen in the context of William Rufus's policy concerning the Scots (Barrow 1973; Kapelle 1979). The northernmost part of the great Anglo-Saxon kingdom of Northumbria had fallen within the sphere of the kings of Scotland, as had been recognised by Edgar's grant to the king of Scots in 945 by which Cumberland in the west and the Lothians in the east were ceded to the king of the Scots. 'English' Northumbria was henceforth restricted to the region south of the Tweed. To the west of the Pennines, Gospatric's charter concerning the Wigton area implies that Earl Siward (d. 1055) had managed to push his lordship northwards through Cumbria to the Solway. These Northumbrian earls were instrumental in re-establishing the dynasty of Duncan, king of Scots (slain by Macbeth in 1040), in the person of Malcolm III (Canmore). Presumably the Northumbrians had intended that Malcolm should be little more than a puppet king, but Malcolm had wider ambitions. He seized the opportunity provided by the fall of Tosti and the subsequent hostility to William the Conqueror in the North to attempt to reunite ancient Northumbria under Scottish lordship. Malcolm therefore annexed the country south of the Tweed and, by 1080, had regained Cumberland and north Westmorland. Relations between the king of the Scots and the king of England were uneasy throughout the 1080s, culminating in Malcolm's fourth invasion of English Northumbria in 1091. This provoked William Rufus's campaign which restored the far North-West to England. Dolfin (presumably Malcolm's vassal) was expelled from Cumbria; Malcolm was killed soon thereafter. After 1092 William Rufus was therefore able to consolidate his position by building a castle at Carlisle and settling loyal followers in the hinterland.

The success of William Rufus's annexation of Cumbria and its absorption into the English kingdom was heavily dependent on there being a reliable network of feudal lordships across north-west England (Barrow 1975). This explains the creation not just of the lordship of Lancaster, but also of the barony of Kendal and the other great feudal baronies of Cumbria. These lordships were parcelled out as large compact baronies which radiated out from the central Lakeland massif (Winchester 1987) and which ultimately formed the basis of the counties of Lancashire, Westmorland and Cumberland.

This concentration of estates in the hands of one person was instrumental in giving a new sense of unity and a new focus for Roger's holdings in the North-West. The 'unity' was to become the honour of Lancaster, and eventually the historic county – though not without challenges to this unity during the troubled reign of Stephen. The new focus was Lancaster (Pl. 10) which became the seat of the honour. In 1086 Lancaster had been a component of the old Lune Valley estate of Halton. The Norman motte-and-bailey castle built there reflects the importance of the place. But after c. 1092, once Roger was having to manage territories either side of the Lune estuary, it clearly made sense to move the administrative centre of the estates downriver, in order to command the lands of Furness and Cartmel, as well as Amounderness. No longer was this region to be run as a part of a wider Northumbrian lordship with its orientation to the east of the Pennines. Now it took on an identity of its own as a new strategic territory based on Lancaster. There were still going to be problems, of course. The lands Between the Ribble and the Mersey, regarded as an apanage of Cheshire for most of two centuries, were obviously going to be difficult to run from Lancaster. Not only were there communication difficulties, but the earls of Chester had a vested interest in them. It is not surprising that the honour retained interests at Salford and West Derby throughout the medieval period.

Amongst Roger of Poitou's first actions on regaining and extending his Lancashire fiefs were the construction of a castle at Lancaster and the endowment of a priory there, a daughter house of St Martin of Séez in France. The former gave a military focus for his fiefs; the latter was to ensure him a place in the hereafter. Both foundations were also status symbols, outward displays of the wealth and power of this great feudal magnate.

In order to fulfil his obligations under knight service Roger enfeoffed a number of sub-tenants. Already by 1086 Roger had begun to do this, and by the time of the compilation of Great Domesday Book there were 8 in West Derby, 7 in Warrington, 2 in Blackburn, 5 in Salford (including Gamel) and 5 in Leyland. No Norman sub-tenants are specified for Newton Hundred. Great efforts have been made to identify these men, an exercise not helped by the fact that several share the same personal name (surnames are rarely given, for they were only just beginning to be used on any scale). We cannot know for certain whether the William who held land in West Derby was the same William who held land in Warrington hundred, though it has been claimed that both entries refer to one and the same William, who is identified with the William fitz Nigel who held land in Cheshire as well. William fitz Nigel's Cheshire holdings included the multi-settlement estate based on Halton castle in 1086 and it is logical to see him as having lands across the Mersey Gap, the precursor of the barony of Widnes. Nor can we say for certain whether either of the Warins holding land in Salford was the same Warin who held land in Warrington, and if so whether he was also the same Warin holding land in West Derby. It is equally uncertain whether there was widespread dispossession of the thanes, etc., who held the unnamed berewicks in 1066. Gamel, who held Rochdale as two hides in 1066, is very probably the same Gamel who held two carucates of land in Salford hundred 'by gift of Roger of Poitou'. It is likely that a good number (allowing for natural wastage) of others stayed on as sub-tenants of the Norman men-at-arms.

Roger may have found a few of his earlier tenants – or their sons – still in place in 1092, though it is probable that some of his earlier tenants (who may have been his personal household knights) lost their holdings when he was dispossessed before 1086. This probably helps to explain why it is so difficult to trace them in the records. Some of these sub-tenants may have exchanged their holdings for tenancies elsewhere on Roger's vast estates; others have dropped out of sight altogether. Albert Grelley (*Greslet*), who was enfeoffed with part of Blackburn Hundred by Roger, is surely an ancestor of the Grelleys who later were enfeoffed with Manchester. Certainly, the likelihood of two different local families bearing the same distinctive surname is rather remote. It has also been claimed that Albert's fellow-tenant in Blackburn, Roger de Busli, is an ancestor of the Bussels of Penwortham. The name does sound similar but is etymologically distinct (McKinlay 1981). Roger de Busli was claimed to have been a relative (*cognatus*) of Robert de Bellême, Roger of Poitou's elder brother. Although they lost their Lancashire lands, the Buslis retained a large holding in Yorkshire which became known as the Barony of Tickhill.

The redistribution of fiefs by first William the Conqueror and then William Rufus in the years before 1092 paved the way for the creation of the honour of Lancaster, though technically the honour belongs to Henry I's time. After the rebellion of Robert Bellême, in which Roger of Poitou was implicated, Henry confiscated all of Roger's Lancashire estates, but they retained their unity and between 1114 and 1116 they were given to Henry's favoured nephew, Stephen Count of Boulogne, the future King Stephen. Stephen held the Honour of Lancaster as tenant-in-chief of the crown. Like his predecessor Roger, he had many Norman connections and it is not surprising that the monastery he founded at Tulketh near Preston was for a group of Savignac monks. The Savignacs were a French order, which later merged with the Cistercians in 1147. The monks only stayed at Tulketh for a short time; within three years they had been removed to Furness where Stephen granted them extensive endowments out of his demesne there. This grant split the southern part of Furness into the land held directly by the monks of Furness and the lands held by Michael le Fleming. Michael's estate (Muchland) lay in the south-eastern part of the peninsula and during the lifetime of the first abbot the respective boundaries were rationalised by exchanges which left the monks with Crivelton and Roose, while Michael had Bardsea and Urswick, manors adjoining his chief manor of Aldingham. There was a dispute over the rights of advowson of

Urswick church, however, and consequently Michael seems to have built his own church on his manor of Aldingham where he established his son, Daniel le Fleming, some time between 1150 and 1180. The further territorial history of Furness shows that the internal boundary divisions of the upland areas of Lancashire were still loosely defined at this period. There is a record of the settling of a boundary dispute on Furness Fell between the demesne holding of the monks of Furness and the Ulverston tenancy of William de Lancaster in 1162 which had the effect of fixing parish boundaries (Farrer 1902: 313). It was agreed that the boundary should run along Thurstan Water, now known as Coniston, William having the western part, which can be mapped as the parish of Ulverston, the monks retaining the land between Coniston and Windermere, the chapelries of Hawkshead and Colton (Fig. 6.5). At around the same time the boundary between the lordship of Furness and de Lancaster's lordship of Kendal was also defined. In future the boundary was to run from Wrynose Haws to Brathay and Windermere (which became the northern boundary of the historic county), and thence followed Windermere to the sea. Cartmel, which was apparently still part of the Honour of Lancaster, was granted to William the Marshall between 1185 and 1186. It was William who founded Cartmel Priory as a house for Augustinian Canons.

On the death of his uncle, Stephen contested the succession to the English throne, opposing Henry's daughter Matilda. The ensuing period of civil war presented David of Scotland with the opportunity to reassert his supremacy over northern England, from which he had been ousted by Rufus in the 1090s. A series of deeds and charters survive to testify to the political intrigues of the middle decades of the twelfth century. David and Stephen entered into an agreement in 1138 whereby Henry, the son of David of Scotland, was promised the earldom of Northumbria in return for the support of Scotland. The Scots interpreted this grant to their favour and sent an army to occupy northern England, including Lancashire as far south as the river Ribble. At the same time Ranulf II, Earl of Chester, one of the most powerful of the English magnates, annexed Lancashire *Inter Mersham et Ripam*. This part of Lancashire had indeed been regarded as a part of Cheshire in the eleventh century, but Ranulf went beyond this and tried to extend his northern boundaries to include the whole honour of

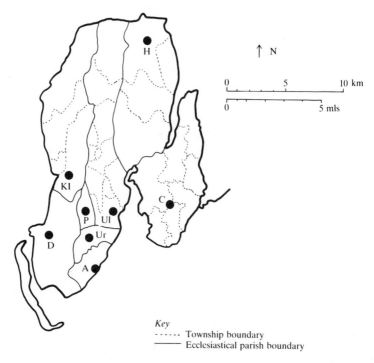

Fig. 6.5 Ecclesiastical parishes in Lancashire North of the Sands

Key A – Aldingham, C – Cartmel, D – Dalton, H – Hawkshead with Colton, detached chapelry belonging to Dalton parish, KI – Kirkby Ireleth, P – Pennington, Ul – Ulverston, Ur – Urswick

Lancaster. By skilful manipulation of the other protagonists Ranulf managed to acquire legal possession of the honour between 1141 and 1149. Ranulf's success over Lancaster was short-lived. According to the terms of the Treaty of Wallingford in 1153 it was agreed that Stephen's only son, William of Mortain, also known as de Warenne, was to hold the honour of Lancaster; the Scots were forced to surrender their claims to Northumbria. On William's death (1159) and the remarriage of his widow the honour reverted back to the crown in 1164. John, brother and heir of Richard the Lionheart, a later count of Mortain, was granted the honour when his brother became king in 1189.

The Honour of Lancaster was in crown hands between 1164 and 1189 and it is during this period of Henry II's reign that one finds the first documentary references to the county or shire of Lancaster as distinct from the honour. Bagley (1976: 32) places the first reference to 1168; Farrer (1902: xvii) noted the first entry in the Pipe Rolls under the year 1182. Up to and including 1182 Lancaster had been included under either Northumberland or Yorkshire; after 1182 a separate heading was entered for the shire of Lancaster. One must be careful to distinguish between the honour and the shire. An honour is essentially a feudal lordship, a collection of manors and castles, of feudal dues and prerequisites, which does not necesssarily have any geographical cohesion. Indeed, some of the estates belonging to the honour of Lancaster lay in other parts of the country, in Derbyshire, Nottinghamshire and Suffolk.

The boundaries of the shire and Norman baronies

One presumes that the area of this twelfth-century shire is the same as that of the ancient county of Lancashire, that is, Lancashire North of the Sands and Lancashire South of the Sands as defined before the boundary changes after the Boundary Commission judgments of 1888 and the Local Government Act of 1894 which transferred Dalton to Westmorland. The boundaries of the county can be fixed along the south and east by reference to the external boundaries of the six hundredal estates south of the Ribble and those of the lordship of Amounderness. In the north the boundary ran from Silverdale to Leck, roughly following the Lune watershed. As the map shows (Fig. 6.4) this boundary ignores the earlier Domesday estates in the area. Nor is it exactly conterminous with units of ecclesiastical administration. The townships of Ireby and Dalton belonged to parishes outside Lancashire and, more significantly, the county boundaries of Lancashire and Westmorland cut right across the rural deanery of Lonsdale.

The Domesday estate of Whittington, as already noted, originally extended into Yorkshire, Westmorland and Lancashire. Bentham, apparently made up of Ketel's holding of Wennington, Tatham, Farleton and Tunstall plus the smaller holdings of Ulf and Orm, was chiefly located within Lancashire, but its *caput*, as well as Thornton, lay across the Yorkshire border as it was later defined. Beetham, which straddled the Kent estuary, was defined on the west side by the River Winster. This formed the boundary with Cartmel and later the county boundary. The land between the Winster and the Kent, together with most of the vills across the Kent, fell into the county of Westmorland. Yealand and Borwick were left in Lancashire. To the east of Beetham most of the Domesday estate of Austwick went to Westmorland, though three vills, including Clapham, were lost to Yorkshire; Warton, Claughton, Caton and Priest Hutton went to Lancashire.

Some of the vills which were found within the later county of Lancashire became single-township parishes, as for example Claughton and Tatham. Others were amalgamated to form the small multi-settlement parish of Warton which was co-extensive with the late twelfth-century fitz Reinfrid lordship. The creation of Warton parish clearly mirrors the post-Conquest pattern of secular lordship in north Lancashire. The same applies to Melling parish, created out of the Domesday estate of Bentham, minus its *caput*, which was tied to the secular Montbegon lordship. Both Hornby (Melling) and Warton developed in what have been identified as mid-first millennium hillfort territories, reflecting the endurance of central place functions and strategic territories over two millennia.

Warton, Hornby and the other Norman baronies begin to appear in surviving documents from the twelfth century onwards (Fig. 6.6). It is clear that there was an ongoing process of exchange and consolidation, manors changing hands through marriage contracts, failure of dynasties, political manoeuvring and so on (VCH I: 291). For example, the Chipping area, often referred to as Chippingdale during this period, was apparently part of the Penwortham fee of Warin Bussel I before 1101, but thereafter appears as part of the Lacy fee of Clitheroe. The de Lancaster fiefs in north Lancashire, acquired after the death of the first Norman tenant, Ivo Taillebois, passed to the Fitz Reinfrid family on the marriage of Gilbert fitz Reinfrid and the de Lancaster heiress, Helewise, in 1184. Farrer suggests that the explanation for the de Lancaster possession of Warton and Garstang lordships may have been kinship between William de Lancaster's wife and the wife of William de Warenne. The surname may derive from their possession of lands in the honour of Lancaster.

As mentioned above, the credit for the creation of the monastic lordship of Furness is given to Stephen. Furness, together with Cartmel, encompass the whole of Lancashire North of the Sands.

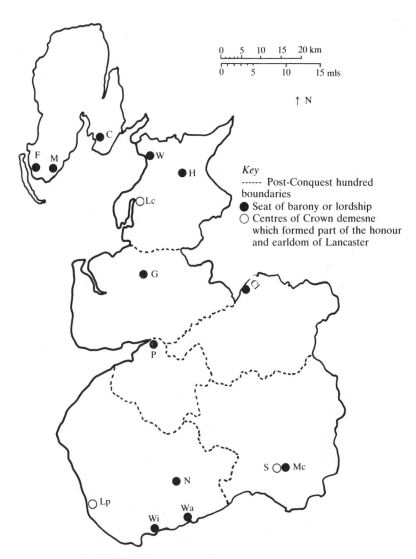

Fig. 6.6 Norman baronies in Lancashire

Key C – Cartmel Priory, Cl – Clitheroe, De Lacy, F – Furness Abbey, G – Garstang, fitz Reinfrid, H – Hornby, Montbegon, Lc – Lancaster, Lp – Liverpool, M – Muchland, le Fleming, Mc – Manchester, Grelley, N – Newton, Banaster, P – Penwortham, Bussel, S – Salford, W – Warton, fitz Reinfrid, Wa – Warrington, Butler, Wi – Widnes fee

They have strong geographical and historical identities arguably going back to the hillfort territories of Skelmore Heads and Castle Head in the first millennium BC. Like many other major Lancashire lordships and baronies, Furness can be closely identified with a Domesday estate, giving a strong thread of continuity for the territorial unit there. Most of the baronies which appear in records from the twelfth century, the Pipe Rolls, for example, and the various inquests – especially the Great Inquest into Knights' Fees of 1212 – can be associated with earlier antecedents. In particular there is a close relationship between Norman baronies and eleventh-century hundreds Between the Ribble and the Mersey. The de Lacy lordship based on Clitheroe is widely regarded as the successor to the hundredal estate of Blackburn, though the full extent of the honour of Clitheroe extended beyond the hundred, including Rochdale in the north-east portion of Salford Hundred, and Chippingdale in the south-east corner of Amounderness. The de Lacy family held considerable lands on the other side of the Pennines, including the great fee of Pontefract. Ilbert de Lacy had acquired the honour of Clitheroe by 1102 but he does not seem to have held any Lancashire estates in 1086. The de Lacys retained Clitheroe for over a century, after which it passed by marriage to the house of Lancaster with all the de Lacy estates.

The core of the honour of Clitheroe's demesne lay around the Clitheroe – Burnley area, and they erected a castle in Clitheroe. The 11 m-square Norman keep, constructed of local limestone, still survives, dominating the little town which grew up outside the castle walls (Pl. 2). During the medieval period castles had more than just a military function. They were the outward symbol of the lord's power, wealth and might, and acted as the main adminis- trative and judicial focus for his territory. The importance of Clitheroe can be seen when one considers its position in relation to the trans-Pennine routes. It dominates the central stretch of the valley of the Ribble near the confluence of the Hodder and Calder, and the castle is obviously located to guard the Ribble–Aire Gap. Clitheroe castle stands at the end of a chronological chain of 'central places' in this part of Lancashire which begins with the defended hilltop site at Portfield, continues though the Anglo- Saxon period at Whalley and Blackburn, and transfers to Clitheroe in post-Conquest times.

The second important barony with a long history of antecedents is Penwortham, the seat of the Bussel family from at least the opening of the twelfth century. The barony is believed to have been created between 1102 and 1118 and the first of the line is usually accepted to have been Warin Bussel I. It has been conjectured that he was one of the Warins holding land in south Lancashire in 1086. The barony of Penwortham encompassed much of Leyland hundred, plus some manors in the Fylde. The military centre of the fief was at Penwortham, where a castle and small urban nucleus of at least six burgages had been established by 1086, perhaps on the site of an Anglo-Saxon *burh*. Today the remains of the motte-and-bailey castle can still be seen on the mound beside the church. There is little trace of the town, which has clearly been supplanted by Preston across the river.

Penwortham church and castle both stand on a spur of land which juts out into the Ribble, emphasising the importance of this stretch of the Ribble as a crossing. Penwortham lies 10 km from the river mouth and today's modern road, the A59, crosses the river a few hundred metres from the castle. The site of the Roman supply base is only around 2 km upstream. The Viking Age Cuerdale hoard was found a little further upriver. As seen in the previous chapter, it may have been Edward's intention to construct a *burh* at Penwortham, to guard against the Ribble estuary being used as an anchorage for the Scandinavian fleet. Like Clitheroe, Penwortham is an example of continuity of central place functioning associated with a communication node which has determined the identity of a strategic territory.

Warrington, the seat of the Butler family, is also clearly associated with an historically important river crossing. A Roman supply depot lay across the river at Wilderspool, and an Anglo-Saxon *burh* was established at nearby Thelwall. After the early years of the tenth century the emphasis shifted to the north bank of the river. Mote Hill, which was the largest motte-and-bailey castle in the county, is the site of the medieval castle of Warrington. Finds from mid-nineteenth-century excavations suggest that the castle lay on an earlier fortifed site. The Butler fee was quite extensive, comprising in all eight knight's fees, five of which lay outside the county, in Lincolnshire, Nottinghamshire and Derbyshire. The manors of the fee of Warrington lay mostly in the east of the Domesday hundred. Richard le Botler (fl. 1149–60) acquired the fee of Warrington through marriage to Beatrice de

Villers, grandaughter of Pain de Villers (fl. *c.* 1100–1120). The Butlers were hereditary butlers to the earls of Chester and whilst Pain probably owes his tenure of Warrington to his good relations with Stephen, the Butler interest surely was dependent on the earls of Chester, who were closely involved in this part of Lancashire in the middle years of the century.

The lower Mersey crossing was very important in post-Conquest times and control was not solely vested in any one family. Control of the Runcorn Gap belonged to Widnes, part of the fee of the Constable of Chester. This important lordship included part of the eleventh-century hundreds of Warrington and West Derby plus Astley in the eastern part of Warrington hundred. (By the end of the twelfth century the hundreds of Newton, Warrington and West Derby had been amalgamated to form one large hundred, West Derby.) The retention of the detached part at Astley may reflect an earlier tradition of exploitation of outlying woodland. The name itself is suggestive of an area which was formerly wooded, and several other 'woodland' place-names like Leigh, Shakerley and Tyldesley lie in the vicinity. With the exception of Astley, Widnes constituted a compact block straddling the old hundred boundaries. This fee of Widnes must, of course, be examined in conjunction with the Constable of Chester's holdings based on Halton castle, on the south bank of the Mersey. Halton was held by William fitz Nigel in 1086 and it is possible that he can be identified with the William who held two hides and four carucates in Warrington and the William who held one and a half hides in West Derby at that date. This pattern of strategic landholding on both sides of the Mersey gap calls to mind the Domesday estate of Uhtred. Uhtred held seventeen manors in West Derby Hundred and, assuming all references were to the same person, also held Wallasey in Wirral and Norton near Halton. The Constable of Chester's holding spanning the river emphasises a point made in Chapter 2: a strategic territory is not necessarily a natural resource territory though the two may overlap.

The Montbegon lordship of Hornby, which has already been touched upon, is yet another strategic estate based on a river crossing, this time in the Lune valley. The impressive earthworks at Castlestede which overlook the fording-place (Pl. 5) are probably the remains of the Norman castle, but may be a re-used Iron Age site. The first recorded member of the Montbegon family to set foot on English soil is Roger de Montbegon, who according to tradition came over to England in the retinue of Roger of Montgomery, perhaps in the household of his son, Roger of Poitou. There is no evidence that the Montbegons held any Lancashire estates of Roger in 1086, though the family held estates of Roger of Poitou in Lincolnshire. Indeed it is unlikely that the Montbegons had an interest in this part of Lancashire until after 1094. For in that year Melling church was included in the endowment of the priory Roger of Poitou had recently founded at Lancaster. Later an agreement was reached whereby Gressingham was transferred to Lancaster parish in exchange for Melling which thereafter formed part of the Hornby fee. Some idea of the extent of the Montbegon holding can be obtained from the Inquest of 1212, when Roger de Montbegon III, lord of Hornby, also held lands at Tottington in Salford Hundred, and at Croston in Leyland Hundred.

The closeness of the ties between the leading barons of Lancashire and the holder of the honour can be seen in the foundation of Hornby Priory. This Praemonstratensian house was founded as a daughter house of Croxton Abbey, Leicestershire, which had itself been jointly founded by William the Porter and William, Count of Mortain, Stephen's son. The social and feudal obligations which bound the magnates to the lord of Lancaster helped to give a unity to the county.

Returning to the southern part of Lancaster there are two major fees still to be discussed, those of Newton and Manchester. The history of the barony of Newton-in-Makerfield was traced by Beaumont in the nineteenth century (1871). Though obviously based on the Domesday Hundred, as far as documentation is concerned its appearance is relatively late. It is first mentioned in Henry II's time when the fee was held by the Banastre family. According to tradition the fee was given to Robert Banastre in compensation for his loss of Prestatyn in North Wales in 1167. Robert brought many of his people with him from North Wales to Lancashire where they were known as 'Les Westroys'. The epithet survives in the place-name Welch Whittle.

Far more is known about the early history of the fee of Manchester, partly due to the work of Tait (1904) and others at the turn of the century. This barony seems to date from just after 1092, the time when Roger of Poitou regained his lands Between the Ribble and the Mersey. Roger – or perhaps Henry I – bestowed extensive landholdings in the hundred of Salford on Robert Grelley I (fl. first half of the twelfth century) who was apparently a descendant of his former Blackburn tenant, Albert de Gresli. The extent of the barony can be reconstructed from various surveys, inquests and rentals. Some manors outside Salford Hundred were held of the barony, including Childwall in West Derby, and lands in Leyland and Warrington. In Salford Hundred the barony formed a fairly compact belt of manors running more or less diagonally from Anglezarke in the north-west to Ashton-under-Lyne in the southeast (Fig. 6.1). To meet their obligations under knight service of twelve knights' fees in Lancashire, the Grelleys created a number of sub-infeudated manors, including Heaton Norris (named from the twelfth-century tenant, the Norreys family), Withington and Ashton. The centre of the titular barony lay at the cathedral end of Deansgate, where the Grelleys are believed to have erected their castle. This seems to have been a fairly small-scale castle, perhaps little more than a fortified manor house, on a platform of high ground overlooking the confluence of the Irk and Irwell. The castle was short-lived: the first mention belongs to the Pipe Roll for 1184 and it disappears from the records after the baronial revolt against King John.

Unlike the situation in Blackburn and Newton, the Grelleys were not the only important landholders in the hundred. As already noted, Gamel's holding, which can be identified with the parish of Rochdale, was regarded as part of the Honour of Clitheroe. Rochdale had its own castle, at Castleton, on a pronounced spur overlooking the valley of the Roch where the later town of Rochdale developed. The Montbegons also had a significant holding in the north of the hundred, Tottington, Bury and Oldham, a belt of manors separating Rochdale from the holding of the baron of Manchester.

Other lands belonged to the manor of Salford. This important manor had been incorporated in the Honour of Lancaster when Henry I created the Honour for his nephew between 1114 and 1116. The manor of Salford included Salford itself and a compact block of manors surrounding the *caput*, as well as Radcliffe (held as demesne by the crown in 1086), Failsworth and land around Bolton. Salford was held for a time by William Peveril, an ally of Stephen, but then fell into the hands of Ranulf II Gernons, earl of

Chester, who assumed the lordship of Salford when he annexed south Lancashire. The earls of Chester regained an interest in the manor during the reign of Henry II, and it was an earl of Chester, Ranulf III Blundeville, who made Salford a free borough by a charter dated 1230. This was some seventy years before the last surviving Grelley gave the already existing urban community at Manchester its charter in 1301. The territory based on Manchester is manifestly in origin a strategic territory. It is a territory associated with control of a strategically important communication node used as a military centre from Roman times. Salford, on the other hand, is perhaps best interpreted as the *caput* of a natural resource territory in the Manchester embayment. As noted above, these territories frequently overlap and in this instance they coalesced to form the hundred of Salford. Over time both Manchester and Salford have developed central place functions of their own, markets and manorial centres, and, latterly, cathedrals and universities. The different histories of Manchester and Salford, and the higher status of the latter's lords in medieval times, help to explain the continued persistence of the duality of Manchester and Salford and the development of the two rival towns on opposite banks of the Irwell. As argued in the previous chapter, the duality may go back at least as far as 919, the time of the construction of the *burh* at Manchester.

The territorial dispositions of that part of Lancashire between the Ribble and the Lune watershed, the post-Conquest hundreds of Amounderness and Lonsdale South of the Sands, reveal an equally complex pattern of parishes and lordship. Two compact blocks of land were held by the fitz Reinfrid family as their lordships of Garstang and Warton. Garstang has tentatively been identified as a tenth-century Scandinavian lordship; Warton developed out of the reorganisation of Domesday estates in north Lancashire already discussed. Most of the remainder of Amounderness and Lonsdale was held of the honour of Lancaster. The geographical core of the honour was Tosti's former estate of Halton, which was in essence yet another strategic territory. It also included a major part of Tosti's former manor of Preston. Only a small part was held in demesne, though besides Lancaster this included Preston, Poulton and Kirkham, three of the most important Domesday manors in Amounderness. The redirection of the focus of Tosti's estate from Halton to Lancaster at the river mouth left a vacuum further up the river. This was filled by the creation of the Montbegon lordship of Hornby (discussed above).

A large part of the honour of Lancaster was granted out in serjeanty, in return for various services designed to assist the lords of the honour in their hunting and at their castle at Lancaster. Halton itself (which became a single township parish) was held by the Gernets as hereditary Master Foresters in Lancashire. They held the manor in return for the service of conveying the lord's foresters everywhere within the county. Other manors, like Middleton, Ellel, Warton (near Preston), Freckleton and Claughton (Fylde) were held in return for castleward at Lancaster castle. By the thirteenth century duty as castleguard was widely accepted as an alternative to military service in the field. In a few instances building work at the castle was required, as at Bowerham, today a suburb of Lancaster. In 1346 the holder of the manor there, William de Bolrun, held by serjeanty of 'coming with one mason for the works at the castle while the lord pleases'. Similarly Thomas de Walton and Alice de Slene, who held the manor of Slyne just to the north of Lancaster, were required to perform, as their serjeanty service, 'reaping and carpentry at the castle'.

Hundred courts and the growth of the boroughs

During the twelfth and thirteenth centuries major centres of lordship developed at Furness, Hornby, Lancaster, Clitheroe, Penwortham, Warrington, Manchester and Salford, with lesser ones at Newton, Warton and Garstang. Each of these soon had their own borough or, in the case of Newton and Garstang, market town, which acted as a market focus for the locality and freqently exercised religious, judicial and administrative functions. The formative years for the development of the historic county experienced a nation-wide increase in borough foundation, and Lancashire was no exception. Furness Abbey had its market town at Dalton, the ancient parish centre. In other places, as at Clitheroe and Lancaster, the town nestled at the foot of the Norman castle. These boroughs and markets were not always successful, however, and the borough of Warton, for example, which is documented between 1244 and 1271, failed.

In some places the hundred courts (or wapentake courts as they were commonly called in Lancashire), which were subordinate to the county court which sat at Lancaster, were merged with baronial courts. This reinforced the importance of places like Clitheroe (de Lacy, Blackburn hundred), Penwortham (Bussels, later de Lacy, Leyland hundred) and Newton (Banastre, later Langton, Newton hundred). Elsewhere, wapentake and baronial courts sat, the latter dealing with cases pertaining to their holdings and tenants within the hundred. In Salford hundred, for example, a wapentake court sat as well as the baronial court leet for the Grelley barony of Manchester. In Amounderness, the barons of Kendal held a baronial court at Garstang. Again this emphasised the local significance of these developing urban centres.

There were four royal boroughs in the county, Lancaster, Preston, Wigan and Liverpool, all located at major communication nodes. The first three were at strategic centres used by the Romans: Lancaster, Walton-le-Dale and Wigan respectively. Liverpool was an entirely new creation founded by King John (see below) to replace the earlier borough associated with the hundredal centre of West Derby. Liverpool began to supplant the central place role of Warrington and Manchester as the major access point for entry to the North-West via the Mersey in the later medieval period, and its success has depended largely on its role as a port. The absence of a Roman presence in the Liverpool area is therefore particularly striking. To some extent this can be explained by the relative isolation of the Liverpool area in ancient times, cut off from the rest of the region by mosses. Yet this did not deter later rulers and one cannot help but wonder if there is a lost Roman site in the vicinity.

It is also interesting to note the emergence of Preston as a royal borough on the north bank of the Ribble. Preston had been the *caput* manor of the lordship of Amounderness and was held after the Conquest as part of the honour of Lancaster rather than being granted out as a barony. In mercantile terms Preston was probably the most prosperous borough in the whole county. Its importance was strengthened after the elevation of Lancashire to the status of county palatine (see below) since Preston became the seat of the chancery for the county palatine; the criminal courts continued to sit at Lancaster. Since at least the eleventh century, therefore, Preston has acted as the meeting-place for the two halves of the shire, north and south of the Ribble. This division arose in the tenth century and has been perpetuated in ecclesiastical terms by the archdeaconries of Richmond (north of the Ribble) and Chester (south of the Ribble.)

Forest

It is noteworthy that the demesne lands included Fulwood, Myerscough and Swainshead in Amounderness, and Hutton (formerly within the Domesday manor of Halton). The exact location of the manor of Hutton is not known but it is believed to have lain in the Quernmore area. These manors together formed the greater part of the demesne forest of Lancaster, the Forests of Fulwood, Myerscough, Over Wyresdale and Quernmore, and explain why the parish of Lancaster included the detached portions of Fulwood and Myerscough (presumably carved out of Preston parish). These vills constituted the forest proper and remained identified as Forest beyond the medieval period (Shaw 1956).

It should be remembered that during the medieval period 'forest' was a legal concept. The term derived from the Latin preposition *foris* meaning 'outside of', and signified that forest land was outside the normal law of the land, subject to its own peculiar system of law, Forest Law. This body of law developed to protect royal hunting rights in designated areas. There were stiff penalties for removing undergrowth, felling *haut bois* (trees like the oak), assarting, keeping hunting dogs, allowing the trespass of cattle, as well as killing the deer. The administration and enforcement of the customs of the forest was the responsibility of the Chief Justice of the Forest. By the time of Henry II, there were two principal justices, one in charge of the Forest North of the Trent, and one for the Forests South of the Trent. Robert Grelley was made Henry III's northern justice in 1225. The office was not abolished until an act of 1817. Beneath the chief justice there were groups of other forest officials, like the Gernets of Halton, who were responsible for particular forest areas.

The forest was originally meant to be a hunting preserve of the king, and as such the concept is pre-Conquest in origin. Under the Normans the practice was formalised and the area subjected to Forest Laws was greatly extended. This is explicitly stated in some Domesday entries, for example those which refer to the lost Domesday vills of *Aldredelie* and *Done* in the hundred of Roelau in Cheshire. Domesday explicitly states that these vills had been placed in the forest of the earl of Chester (*est modo in foresta comitis*), which became known as Delamere Forest. There are no directly comparable entries for Lancashire, though one suspects that the lost vill of *Aschebi* in Amounderness suffered a similar fate. It is thought that the vill lay in the Myerscough area which was forest belonging to the Honour of Lancaster. *Wibaldeslei*, a lost vill in West Derby Hundred, may have been incorporated into the forest of West Derby. Significantly, the last part of the place-name is Old English **lēah** rather than **tūn**. **Lēah** means '(a settlement in) a lightly wooded area', whereas **tūn** would normally be used in cleared areas. A large area of forest (*foresta*), 2 leagues long and 1 league wide, belonged to King Edward's demesne manor of West Derby and this is likely to have formed the basis of the forest of the later Honour of Lancaster in that hundred. King Edward also had extensive forest in Salford Hundred, 3 leagues long and 1 league wide, belonged to King Edward's demesne manor estates in these two hundreds *Inter Ripam et Mersham* after the conquest. These estates were later incorporated into the Honour of Lancaster rather than forming parts of Norman baronies.

It is unlikely that these areas of royal forest predate the crown acquisition of south Lancashire after the execution of Wulfric Spot's heirs. On the Continent attempts have been made to demonstrate a specialised use of **feld** to denote 'a clearing with a royal hunting station' (Nitz 1988) during the Ottonian period. Such place-names are particularly associated with the medieval royal Harz Forest. In north-west England **feld** can occasionally be associated with medieval forests. This is best exemplified by Macclesfield Forest. Hundersfield in Rochdale Parish, within the confines of Rossendale Forest, is another example. Unfortunately there is as yet little evidence to suggest a systematic association of **feld** place-names with hunting lodges, though further study may show otherwise (e.g. Higham 1989). The correlation between **feld** names and forests, where it exists, seems to be best explained by the use of former common grazing land, or **feld**-land, on the Pennine foothills as hunting grounds. Indeed, the men of Lancaster were still claiming ancient rights of common grazing in Quernmore Forest in the medieval period.

In the immediate post-Conquest period the areas of forest, or more properly seigneurial chase, was relatively small in Lancashire. Very soon, however, an extensive belt of surrounding vills were included within the metes and bounds of the forests, to the great distress of local lords and of the local population generally. These vills were known collectively as the *purlieu* of the forest and were subject to the same general restrictions concerning the hunting of game. The initial reason for incorporating these vills within the forest is thought to have been to discourage poachers rather than to raise money through the levying of fines or to punish the inhabitants, as was reputedly the case when the Wirral in Cheshire was afforested. The Forest of Lancaster was further extended in the fourteenth century when the second earl of Lancaster acquired the Honour of Clitheroe after his marriage to the de Lacy heiress. This added a large part of east Lancashire, which had previously been private chases. It included the chases of Blackburnshire and Tottington. It is interesting to note that the de Lacy chases of Bowland were also added to the Forest of Lancaster by this inheritance in a move which prefigures the boundary changes of 1974 when this part of the West Riding of Yorkshire was added to Lancashire.

Parish structure and ecclesiastical organisation

The pattern of landholding as reconstructed from the Great Inquest of 1212 is to some extent reflected in the structure of the pre-Reformation parishes. As noted at the beginning of the chapter, however, some reflect earlier pre-Conquest divisions, as indeed do the major ecclesiasical boundaries of the archdeaconries of Richmond and Chester which meet at the Ribble, and the rural deaneries of Furness, Amounderness, Blackburn, Manchester (Salford hundred) and Leyland. On the other hand, the rural deanery of Warrington can be equated with the post-Conquest hundred of West Derby formed by the amalgamation of the Domesday hundreds of Warrington, Newton and West Derby. Similarly, Lonsdale deanery owes as much to territorial dispositions immediately after the Conquest as to the early eleventh-century pattern. Kendal deanery, which included parts of Bolton-le-Sands, Halton, Heysham and Warton, can clearly be associated with the post-Conquest barony of Kendal and especially with the fitz Reinfrid holdings in north Lancashire.

In the case of individual parishes, Gamel's holding of Rochdale is the most obvious example of a pre-Conquest unit, and the crown

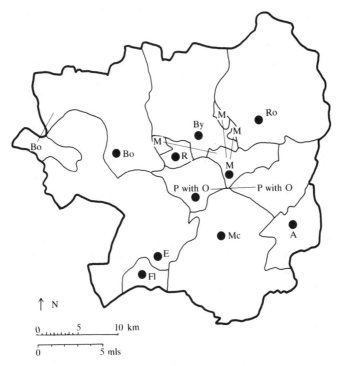

Fig. 6.7 Ecclesiastical parishes in Salford hundred

Key A – Ashton-u-Lyne, Bo – Bolton, By – Bury, E – Eccles, Fl – Flixton, M – Middleton, Mc – Manchester, P with O – Prestwich with Oldham, R – Radcliffe, Ro – Rochdale

demesne manor of Radcliffe, a rare single-parish township, is another (Fig. 6.7). The parish of Ashton can be associated with the manor there. Ashton was granted out by the Grelleys in two stages, half being given to Urm, son of Eiward, when he married Emma, daughter of Albert Grelley (fl. 1154–62), and the other half being given to Orm and Emma's son Roger. If the interpretation of the Domesday entry is correct, and the church of St Michael is Ashton church, then it may be that Ashton is another pre-Conquest unit, though perhaps not of any great antiquity. The small parish of Flixton represents the sub-infeudated manor of Flixton, bestowed on Henry, son of Siward, by the same Albert

Grelley in the middle of the twelfth century. There is no evidence for any pre-Conquest church at Flixton and it may be that this is a later manorial foundation. When one looks at the map, it can be seen that the parish seems to have been carved out of Eccles parish. The relationship between Eccles parish and Manchester parish was discussed in Chapter 4, where it was argued that Manchester once formed part of a much larger parish based on Eccles before 919.

This development of parishes, the fragmentation of large pre-Conquest parishes and the creation of new post-Conquest 'manorial' parishes is repeated across the county. Examples of this include Furness where Michael le Fleming established his church at Aldingham and Gamel erected a church at Pennington. The parish of Ulverston represented the de Lancaster interest, whilst the monks of Furness retained the 'mother' church of Urswick, Dalton and the detached chapelries between Coniston and Windermere (Fig. 6.5). Similar examples can be instanced from elsewhere across the county, especially near the northern border, where Whittington and other small parishes catered for the truncated remains of formerly larger eleventh-century multi-settlement estates. Sometimes estate components were combined to give new groupings. The six townships in the de Reinfrid lordship of Warton, for example, belonged to three separate Domesday estates. The coherence of this estate and its conterminous parish is clearly a post-Conquest development, though one cannot rule out the possibility that it is really a reversion to an earlier teritorial unit. Elsewhere there are detached portions of parishes. Some, like Goosnargh and Whittingham, the detached portion of Kirkham parish, perpetuate early patterns of landscape exploitation. Detached portions of Lancaster parish, however, are more likely to represent areas incorporated into the Forest of Lancaster after the Norman Conquest.

From honour to county palatine

The honour of Lancaster had been held by the crown since 1164. Richard I, who succeeded his father in 1189, then bestowed the honour on his brother John. John took a personal interest in Lancashire, confirming the borough privileges of Preston and Lancaster as well as establishing a new borough at Liverpool. This marks the tentative beginnings of the port's great maritime history. The first surviving charter is dated to around 1206–07, and it is clear that people were encouraged to move from the demesne manor of West Derby to populate the new borough over a period of three years. A large stone castle was subsequently built there, replacing the motte and bailey at West Derby which was reportedly in ruins by 1296. Liverpool, it may be noted, had not originally constituted part of the Lancaster demesne but had been acquired in exchange for Litherland.

This stretch of the Mersey coast has little obvious history of use as a port or even as a harbourage. Earlier activity, apart from the *burh* at Runcorn in Cheshire, had been concentrated along the Warrington stretch of the river where both the Romans and the Anglo-Saxons had their bases. The main springboards for west coast trade, and especially for the Irish Sea trade in this part of the North-West, had been the Dee: Chester was the principal port and Meols on the Wirral coast acted as a beachhead trading centre or *emporium*. John favoured a Lancashire base to free him from reliance on the Earl of Chester for access to the port of Chester for shipping to Ireland where John's principal lordship lay. The selection of Liverpool rather than a site further inland towards Warrington is probably related to the size of the ships then in use. The log-boats found near Warrington had a very shallow draft and were really only suited to the inland stretch of the waterway. The seagoing vessels for the Irish Sea crossing would have needed the deeper anchorage provided by Liverpool.

Under Henry III, the honour of Lancaster was run by a sheriff on the crown's behalf. Lancaster was an important shrievalty and a source of rivalry amongst leading barons. The earls of Chester, who had a long-standing territorial interest in the honour, had held the office under John, but Ranulf III lost the honour during Henry's minority and the shrievalty passed into the hands of the Ferrers family, who were then earls of Derby. Young Robert Ferrers was associated with Simon de Montfort in the baronial movement for reform. After Henry III was restored to power in the summer of 1266, he used the lands and offices which had fallen to the crown as escheats and established his younger son Edmund as one of the most powerful men in the land. Before long Edmund held the possessions of Simon de Montfort, former Earl of Leicester, including the earldom and lands in a dozen

G

counties which had been confiscated after Simon's death. These had been given to Edmund by January 1267. Besides these he was granted the possessions of Robert Ferrers, Earl of Derby, which included Tutbury and Duffield in Derbyshire and, of course, the lands that Robert held in Lancashire. Kenilworth Castle and various estates in Wales, including Monmouth, were also given to Edmund. Finally, by a grant dated 30 June 1267, the honour, county town and castle of Lancaster, together with all royal demesne in the county and the wastes and forests of Wyresdale, were bestowed on Edmund. No formal grant of an accompanying title appears to have been made, but Edmund was known as Earl of Lancaster by around 1280.

This important series of grants of honours, offices and lands to the young Edmund after 1265 established the landed base of what was to become the Duchy of Lancaster. It has been calculated that Edmund, the first earl, held property in 632 places in England and Wales, including 49 demesne manors and 5 castles, and was responsible for the service of 263½ knights' fees (Somerville 1953). His holdings stretched from Dunstanburgh in the Northern Marches to South Wales, though the main concentration was in the counties of Derbyshire, Staffordshire, Leicestershire and Northamptonshire. These lands were augmented by a further significant addition when his mother's gift of a manor in London was confirmed. This manor had been the property of Queen Eleanor's uncle, Peter, Count of Savoy. It was here that the first duke built his palace, known as the Savoy, from which the administration of the Duchy was to be conducted until the present century. Another major addition came about as a result of the advantageous marriage of Edmund's son, Thomas, who became the second earl of Lancaster on his father's death in 1296. Thomas married Alice de Lacy, daughter and heir of Henry de Lacy, Earl of Lincoln. The marriage took place in 1294 (when she was thirteen), and Henry de Lacy and his wife surrendered title to their estates, retaining only a life interest, in favour of Thomas and Alice. On Henry's demise in 1311, Thomas thereby succeeded to the earldoms of Lincoln and Salisbury and to the four de Lacy honours, Pontefract, Bolingbroke, Clitheroe and Halton (Cheshire). This made Thomas the most powerful magnate in the kingdom, second only to the king whom he rivalled in landed wealth.

Forty years later, Henry, the fourth earl, was made a duke and at the same time Edward III raised Lancaster to a county palatine. Initially this grant was only temporary, for the life of the grantee, but John of Gaunt succeeded in obtaining recognition of palatinate powers for himself and his heirs. The elevation of Lancaster to the status of a county palatine is in some ways anachronistic for the middle of the fourteenth century. It reversed the trend of earlier medieval monarchs who had sought to curtail individual liberties and franchises which could pose a challenge to the authority of the crown. One of the main reasons that Lancaster was elevated was because of the strategic position of the county, especially with regard to the war against the Scots. For despite attempts by the first two Edwards, relations with Scotland remained a major problem and there had been serious raiding across northern England in 1316 and again in 1322.

The award of palatinate status conferred legal recognition of the extraordinary regalian powers of the new duke within Lancashire-though it actually cost the impoverished crown very little. Henceforth the county developed its own chancery, issuing writs under its own seal, and even had its own dating year, running from 6 March 1351, the date of the establishment of the palatine. The duke was able to appoint his own sheriff who was answerable to the duke, not to the king. Lancaster had its own justices and the king's writ did not run within the palatine county. The king did, however, reserve the right to levy direct taxation and to correct 'errors of judgement' in the duke's courts. He allowed parliamentary representation from the boroughs and the shire. The palatine of Lancaster therefore differed from the county palatine of Chester, the model on which it was created, in respect of these two last-mentioned aspects. Outside the palatinate, elsewhere on the duchy estates, these special privileges did not apply. The office of Chancellor of the Duchy was quite distinct from the Chancellor of the County Palatine, though confusion often arose because the same person sometimes held both posts. To reduce confusion, two distinct seals were used, a red one for ordinary duchy instruments, a white (or uncoloured) one for palatinate documents. Again one has to be careful to distinguish between the duchy and the county palatine. Palatine powers only applied within the boundaries of the county ('Within the Lyme'), whereas the duchy encompassed holdings dispersed widely across the country, in the North Marches,

South Wales and in the Midlands. Although the duke held regalian powers in Lancashire, where his sheriff and other officials were answerable only to the duke, elsewhere within the duchy ('Beyond the Lyme') the king's writ still ran.

After Henry Bolingbroke became Henry IV in 1399 he kept his Lancastrian patrimony separate from crown lands. Since the duchy was vested in the monarch the palatinate posed no threat to crown authority, and its survival was assured. The county palatine retained its own chancery and judiciary. Statute law and common law had equal authority in the palatine and in the king's courts, a factor which helps to explain the retention of its separate judicial administration (Bagley 1976: 40) until 1873. Prior to then there had been three courts within the county palatine, the court of criminal justice, the court of Common Pleas (which dealt with civil suits) and the court of Chancery (which dealt with pleas of Equity). The three courts largely superseded the former system based on the county, wapentake (hundred) and baronial courts. After the Judicature Act of 1873, however, the court of Common Pleas which had been accustomed to sit at Lancaster was abolished, and both civil and criminal justice were brought under the supervision of the new central high court of justice. The court of Chancery, which had sat at Preston since the fifteenth century (though later sessions were also held at Manchester and Liverpool) continued until 1974.

Conclusion

The origin of the shire of Lancaster is firmly grounded in patterns of territorial organisation which have developed over the millennia. These territories have taken different forms and have been determined by different factors. Natural resource territories developed as earlier communities sought to optimise their exploitation of the landscape. Strategic territories developed around river crossings and other communication nodes. Sometimes these successive territories coincided or overlapped, but not always. Within them central places developed as the foci for estate administration and lordship. Where an estate was essentially based on landed resources, central places or *capita* functioned as administrative centres for the management of the estate and its constituent settlements. Such *capita* would tend to be sited in a lowland part of the estate with ready access to the main arable components. Whenever strategic reasons prevailed then the choice of central place would be determined by considerations of defence and control of communication nodes. Not surprisingly, even though centuries and even millennia separate the use of central place locations, there is a persistent underlying continuity of function. Many of these strategic central places have become centres of modern conurbations. The two Anglican diocesan centres of Manchester and Liverpool, which formed the nuclei of metropolitan counties after 1974, are especially important. But one should not forget Preston, which still has administrative responsibility for the shire county, a role recently reinforced by the decision to build a major new court complex to serve the whole county. Nor should one forget Lancaster, the titular county town, and Blackburn, the third Anglican diocesan see of the county. The success of these central places can be contrasted with the lack of development at sites like Hornby and Whalley. The reasons for this are manifold, but of paramount importance is the role of industry and commerce, especially from the eighteenth century onwards: coal and cotton in south-east Lancashire, and overseas trade via Lancaster, Preston, Liverpool, and, with the opening of the Manchester Ship Canal in 1894, via Manchester.

The historic county of Lancashire into being at a time when the need for strategic territorial lordships and strategically located central places was paramount. This had the effect of re-creating Norman baronies as strategic territories. These territories had a unity imposed from above, a unity which was reinforced by the network of social and feudal obligations which bound together the feudal magnates. Roger of Poitou is often seen as the founder of the historic county, but he was building on a tradition of lordship and estates which predates not only the Normans but also the Anglo-Saxons. Under Roger of Poitou there began the unification of the territorial units North and South of the Sands and north and south of the Ribble, a unity based on his new castle at Lancaster. Within 200 years Lancashire, the last of the English counties to emerge, was elevated to a county palatine. Today the Queen is the Duke of Lancaster. In the words of the toast of loyal Lancastrians everywhere:

'The Duke, God Bless Her.'

Bibliography

Abbreviations used in the bibliography

BAR	British Archaeological Reports
(Brit./Int./Supp. Ser.	British/International/Supplementary Series)
CS	Chetham Society
CW	*Transactions of the Cumberland and Westmorland Antiquarian and Archaeological Society*
HSLC	*Transactions of the Historic Society of Lancashire and Cheshire*
JEPNS	*Journal of the English Place-Name Society*
LCAS	*Transactions of the Lancashire and Cheshire Antiquarian Society*
ns	new series
os	old series
RSLC	Record Society of Lancashire and Cheshire

Aaby, B. (1976) 'Cyclic climatic variations in climate over the past 5,500 years reflected in raised bogs', *Nature*, **263**, 281–4.

Atkin, M. A. (1983) 'Stock tracks along township boundaries', *JEPNS*, **15**, 24–32.

Atkinson, J. C. & Brownbill, J. (1898–1908, 1915–16, 1919) *The Coucher Book of Furness Abbey*, CS, ns 9, 11, 14, 74, 76, 78.

Austin, D. (1985) 'Dartmoor and the upland village of the south west of England', in Hooke 1985, pp. 71–80.

Bagley, J. J. (1976) *A History of Lancashire*, Phillimore.

Bailey, R. N. (1981) *Viking Age Sculpture in Northern England*, Collins.

Banks, H. (1936) 'Blackpool coast defence works', in *A Scientific Survey of Blackpool and District*, ed. A. Grime, British Association for the Advancement of Science, pp. 94–103.

Barrow, G. W. S. (1973) *The Kingdom of the Scots*, Arnold.
Barrow, G. W. S. (1975) 'The pattern of lordship and feudal settlement in Cumbria', *Jnl Medieval History*, **1**, 117–38.
Bassett, S. (ed.) (1989) *The Origins of Anglo-Saxon Kingdoms*, Leicester University Press.
Beaumont, W. (1871) 'The Fee of Makerfield, I', *HSLC*, ns, **12**, 81–130.
Beck, J. (1953) 'The church brief for the inundation of the Lancashire coast, 1720', *HSLC*, **105**, 91–106.
Bendelow, V. C. & Hartnup, R. (1980) *Climatic classification of England and Wales*, Soil Survey Technical Monograph, 15.
Beswick, P. & Coombs, D. G. (1986) 'Excavations at Portfield, hillfort, 1960, 1970 and 1972', in *Archaeology of the Pennines, Studies in Honour of Arthur Raistrick*, ed. G. Manby and P. Turnbull, BAR Brit. Ser., 158, pp. 137–80.
Bird, J. (1977) 'African slipware in Roman Britain', in *Roman Pottery Studies in Britain and Beyond*, ed. J. Dore and K. Greene, BAR Supp. Ser., 30, pp. 269–77.
Birks, H. J. B. (1965) 'Pollen analytical investigations at Holcroft Moss, Lancashire, and Lindow Moss, Cheshire', *Jnl Ecology*, **53**, 299–314.
Brodie, I. O. (1990) 'Landscape and landuse conflict in the Forest of Bowland AONB', in *Field Excursions in North West England*, ed. C. Park, University of Lancaster and Cicerone Press, pp. 188–96.
Buckalzsch, E. J. (1950–51) 'The geographical distribution of wealth in England 1086–1843', *Economic History Review*, 2nd ser., **3**, 180–202.
Bu'lock, J. D. (1956) 'The lost kingdom of Teyrnllwg', *LCAS*, **66**, 38–50.
Caird, J. (1968) *English Agriculture 1850–51*, J. Cass.
Cameron, K. (1965) *Scandinavian Settlement in the Territory of the Five Boroughs: the Place-Name Evidence*, Inaugural Lecture, University of Nottingham.
Cameron, K. (1970) 'Scandinavian settlement in the territory of the Five Boroughs: the place-name evidence, part II, place-names in Thorp', *Medieval Scandinavia*, **3**, 35–49.
Cameron, K. (1971) 'Scandinavian Settlement in the territory of the Five Boroughs: the place-name evidence, part III, the Grimston Hybrids', in *England Before the Conquest: Studies in Primary Sources presented to Dorothy Whitelock*, ed. P. Clemoes and K. Hughes, Cambridge University Press, pp. 147–63.
Cameron, K. (1980) 'The meaning and significance of Old English **walh** in English place-names', *JEPNS* **12**, 1–46.
Chadwick, N. K. (1970) 'Early literary contacts between Wales and Ireland', in *The Irish Sea Province in Archaeology and History*, ed. D. Moore, University of Wales Press, Cardiff, pp. 66–77.
Chapman, J. C. & Mytum, J. C. (eds.) (1983) *Settlement in North Britain 1,000–AD 1,000*, BAR Brit. Ser., 118.
Coatsworth, E. (1983) 'The Angel Stone', in Morris 1983, pp. 9–12.
Colgrave, B. (1927) *The Life of Bishop Wilfrid by Eddius Stephanus*, Cambridge University Press.

Bibliography

Colgrave, B. & Mynors, R. A. B. (1967) *Bede's Ecclesiastical History of the English People*, Oxford University Press.
Collingwood, W. G. (1924) 'The Angles in Furness and Cartmel', *CW*, ns, **24**, pp. 288–94.
Collingwood, W. G. (1927) *Northumbrian Crosses*, Faber & Gwyer.
Collins, H. C. (1953) *Lancashire Plain and Seaboard*, Dent.
Coombs, D. G. (1982) 'Excavations at the hillfort of Castercliff, Nelson, Lancashire, 1970–71', *LCAS*, **81**, 111–30.
Cramp, R. J. (1979) 'The Anglian tradition in the ninth century', in *Anglo-Saxon and Viking Age Sculpture*, ed. J. Lang, BAR, Brit. Ser., 49, pp. 1–32.
Crowe, P. R. (1962) 'Climate', in *Manchester and its Region*, ed. C. F. Carter, British Association for the Advancement of Science, pp. 17–46.
Dickinson, W. (1975) 'Recurrence surfaces in Rusland Moss, Cumbria (formerly North Lancashire)', *Jnl Ecology*, **63**, 913–35.
Dobson, J. (1907) 'Urswick Stone Walls', *CW*, ns, **7**, 72–94.
Dornier, A. (ed.) (1977) *Mercian Studies*, Leicester University Press.
Dornier, A. (1982) 'The Province of Valentia', *Britannia*, **13**, 253–60.
Edwards, B. J. N. (1978) 'An annotated check-list of Pre-Conquest sculpture in the ancient county of Lancashire', *Lancs. Archaeol. Jnl*, **1**, 53–82.
Ekwall, E. (1922) *The Place-Names of Lancashire*, CS, ns, 81.
Ekwall, E. (1964) *Old English* **wīc** in Place-Names, Nomina Germanica, 13.
Farrer, W. (ed.) (1898–1909) *The Chartulary of Cockersand Abbey*, CS, ns, 38–40, 43, 56–7, 64.
Farrer, W. (1898) 'Notes on the Domesday Survey of the land between Ribble and Mersey', *LCAS*, **16**, 1–38.
Farrer, W. (1900) 'Notes on the Domesday Survey of North Lancashire and adjacent parts of Cumberland, Westmorland and Yorkshire', *LCAS*, **18**, 88–113.
Farrer, W. (1902) *Lancashire Pipe Rolls*, Henry Young & Sons, Liverpool.
Farrer, W. (1903) *Lancashire Inquests, Extents, and Feudal Aids 1205–1307*, RSLC, 48.
Farrer, W. *et al.* (eds.) (1906–14) *The Victoria History of the County of Lancaster*, Constable.
Faull, M. L. (1977) 'British survival in Anglo-Saxon Northumbria', in *Studies in Celtic Survival*, ed. L. Laing, BAR Brit. Ser., 37, pp. 1–55.
Faull, M. L. (1980) 'Place-names and the kingdom of Elmet', *Nomina*, **4**, 21–3.
Faull, M. L. & Moorhouse, S. A. (1981) *West Yorkshire: An Archaeological Survey to AD 1500*, West Yorkshire Metropolitan County Council.
Fell, J. (1884) 'The guide over the Kent and Leven Sands, Morecambe Bay', *CW*, **7**, 27–47.
Fellows-Jensen, J. (1972) 'Place-name research and northern history', *Northern History*, **8**, 1–23.

Fellows-Jensen, J. (1978a) *Scandinavian Settlement Names in the East Midlands*, Kommission hos Akademisk forlag Navnestudier udgivet af Institut for Navneforskning.

Fellows-Jensen, J. (1978b) 'A Gaelic–Scandinavian loan-word in English place-names', *JEPNS*, **10**, 18–25

Fellows-Jensen, J. (1983) 'Scandinavian settlement in the Isle of Man and Northern England: the place-name evidence', in *The Viking Age in the Isle of Man*, ed. C. E. Fell, P. G. Foote, J. Graham-Campbell and R. L. Thomson, Viking Society for Northern Research, pp. 37–52.

Fellows-Jensen, J. (1985) *Scandinavian Settlement Names in the North West*, Kommission hos Akademisk forlag Navnestudier udgivet af Institut for Navneforskning.

Fishwick, H. (1898) 'Places in Lancashire destroyed by the sea', *HSLC*, **49**, 87–96.

Fletcher, M. (1986) 'A fortified site at Castle Steads, Walmersley, Bury', *Greater Manchester Archaeol. Jnl*, **2**, 31–40.

Forde-Johnston, J. (1962) 'The Iron Age hillforts of Lancashire and Cheshire', *LCAS*, **72**, 9–46.

Freeman, T. W., Rodgers, H. B. & Kinvig, R. H. (1966) *Lancashire, Cheshire, the Isle of Man*, Nelson.

Freke, D. J. (1982) 'An unsuspected pre-Conquest church and cemetery at Winwick, Cheshire', *Council for British Archaeology Churches Newsletter*, July, pp. 7–8.

Garlick, T. (1970) *Romans in the Lake Counties*, Dalesman (Clapham, Yorks).

Gelling, M. (1974) 'Some notes on Warwickshire place-names', *Trans. Birmingham and Warwickshire Archaeol. Soc.*, **85**, 59–79.

Gelling, M. (1978, repr. 1987) *Signposts to the Past*, Dent.

Gelling, M. (1984) *Place-Names in the Landscape*, Dent.

Gelling, M. (1989) 'The early history of western Mercia', in Bassett, pp. 184–201.

Graham-Campbell, J. (1982) 'Viking silver hoards: an introduction', in *The Vikings*, ed. R. T. Farrer, Phillimore, pp. 32–41.

Graham-Campbell, J. (1987) 'Some archaeological reflections on the Cuerdale hoard', in Metcalf 1987a, pp. 329–44.

Grant, E. (ed.) (1986) *Central Places, Archaeology, and History*, Department of Archaeology and Prehistory, University of Sheffield.

Gresswell, R. K. (1953) *Sandy Shores in South Lancashire*, Liverpool University Press.

Hall, B. R. & Folland, C. J. (1970) *Soils of Lancashire*, Soil Survey Bulletin, 5.

Hallam, J. (1986) *The Surviving Past, Archaeological Finds and Excavations in Central Lancashire*, Central Lancashire New Town Development Corporation.

Hanson, W. S. & Campbell, D. B. (1986) 'The Brigantes: from clientage to conquest', *Britannia,* **17**, 73–90.

Hart, C. (1977) 'The kingdom of Mercia', in Dornier 1977, pp. 43–61.

Hartley, B. R. & Fitts, R. L. (1988) *The Brigantes*, Alan Sutton.

Hibbert, F. A., Switsur, V. R., & West R. G (1971) 'Radio-carbon dating of Flandrian pollen zones at Red Moss, Lancs', *Proceedings of the Royal Society, London, B*, **177**, 161–76.

Higham, M. C. (1978) 'The **erg** place-names of Northern England', *JEPNS*, **10**, 7–17.

Higham, N. J. (ed.) (1979) *The Changing Past*, University of Manchester Department of Extra-Mural Studies.

Higham, N. J. (1986) *The Northern Counties*, Longman.

Higham, N. J. (1987) 'Brigantia revisited', *Northern History*, **23**, 1–19.

Higham, N. J. (1988) 'The Cheshire *burhs* and the Mercian frontier to 924', *LCAS*, **85**, 193–222.

Higham, N. J. (1989) 'Forest, woodland and settlement in medieval Cheshire: a note', *Medieval Settlement Research Group, Annual Report*, **4**, 24–5.

Higham, N. J. & Jones, G. D. B. (1975) 'Frontiers, forts and farmers, Cumbrian aerial survey, 1974–5', *Archaeological Jnl*, **132**, 16–53.

Higham, N. J. & Jones, G. D. B. (1985) *The Carvetti*, Alan Sutton.

Hooke, D. (1985) *Medieval Villages*, Oxford University Council for Archaeology, Monograph, 5.

Hooke, D. (1986) 'Territorial organisation in the Anglo-Saxon West Midlands', in Grant, pp. 79–93.

Hooke, D. (ed.) (1988) *Anglo-Saxon Settlements*, Blackwell, including by the editor, 'Regional variation in southern and central England in the Anglo-Saxon period and its relationship to land units and settlement', pp. 123–51.

Hulton, W. A. (1847–49) *The Coucher Book of Whalley Abbey*, CS, os, 10, 11, 16, 20.

Hulton, W. A. (1853) *History of Penwortham*, CS, os, 30.

Jackson, K. H. (1953) *Language and History in Early Britain*, Edinburgh University Press.

Johnson, R. H. (1985) *The Geomorphology of North-west England*, Manchester University Press.

Jones, G. D. B. (1968) 'The Romans in the North West', *Northern History*, **3**, 1–26.

Jones G. D. B. (ed. S. Grealey) (1974) *Roman Manchester*, John Sherratt & Son (Altrincham) for the Manchester Excavation Committee.

Jones, G. D. B. & Shotter, D. C. A. (1988) *Roman Lancaster*, Brigantia Monograph, 1.

Jones, G. D. B. & Walker, J. (1983) 'Either side of Solway. Towards a minimalist view of Romano-British agricultural settlement in the north west', in Chapman and Mytum, pp. 185–204.

Jones, G. R. J. (1961) 'Early territorial organisation in England and Wales', *Geografiske Annaler*, **43**, 174–81.

Jones, G. R. J. (1975) 'Early territorial organisation in Gwynedd and Elmet', *Northern History*, **10**, 3–27.

Jones, G. R. J. (1976) 'Multiple estates and early settlement', in Sawyer, pp. 15–40.

Jones, I. P. (1976) 'White Moss, Yorkshire', in 'Birmingham University

Bibliography

Radiocarbon dates, X', *Radiocarbon*, **18**, 249–67, especially 255–6.

Radiocarbon dates, X', *Radiocarbon*, **18**, 249–67, especially 255–6.

Kapelle, W. E. (1979) *The Norman Conquest of the North*, Croom Helm.

Kendrick, T. (1852–53) 'An account of excavations made at the Mote Hill, Warrington', *HSLC*, **5**, 59–68.

Kenyon, D. (1985) 'Addenda and corrigenda to E. Ekwall, "The Place-Names of Lancashire"', *JEPNS*, **17**, 20–106.

Kenyon, D. (1986a) 'Notes on Lancashire place-names, 1, the early names', *JEPNS*, **18**, 13–37.

Kenyon, D. (1986b) 'The antiquity of **hām** place-names in Lancashire and Cheshire', *Nomina*, **10**, 11–27.

Kenyon, D. (1986c) 'Danish settlement in Greater Manchester', *Greater Manchester Archaeol. Jnl*, **2**, 63–6.

Kenyon, D. (1989) 'Notes on Lancashire place-names, 2, the later names', *JEPNS*, **21**, 23–53.

King, C. A. M. (1976) *Northern England*, Methuen.

Kirby, D. P. (1965) 'The Battle of Whalley', *HSLC*, **117**, 181–4.

Kirby, D. P. (1987) 'Northumbria in the ninth century', in Metcalf 1987a, pp. 11–25.

Klein, J. *et al.* (1982) 'Calibration of radiocarbon dates', *Radiocarbon*, **24**, 103–50.

Lamb, H. H. (1977) *Climate, Present, Past and Future*, Methuen.

Lang, J. T. (1984) 'The hogback. A Viking colonial monument', in *Anglo-Saxon Studies in Archaeology and History*, 5, ed. S. C. Hawkes, J. Campbell and D. Brown, pp. 85–176.

Lewis, P. (forthcoming).

Longworth, I. H. (1967) 'A Bronze Age hoard from Portfield Farm, Whalley, Lancashire', *British Museum Quarterly*, **32**, 1–2, 8–14.

Lowndes, R. A. C. (1963) 'Celtic fields, farmsteads and burial mounds in the Lune valley', *CW*, ns, **63**, 77–95.

McGrail, S. (ed.) (1979) *The Archaeology of Medieval Ships and Harbours in Northern Europe*, BAR Int. Ser., 66, including by the editor (with R. Switsur), 'Medieval logboats of the River Mersey: a classification study', pp. 93–115.

McKinlay, R. (1981) *The Surnames of Lancashire*, English Surnames Series, 4.

Mason, J. F. A. (1963) 'Roger de Montgomery and his sons', *Trans. Royal Historical Soc.*, 5th ser., **13**, 1–28.

Meaney, A. L. S. (1964) *A Gazetteer of Early Anglo-Saxon Burial Sites*, Allen & Unwin.

Metcalf, D. M. (ed.) (1987a) *Coinage in Ninth Century Northumbria*, BAR Brit. Ser., 180.

Metcalf, D. M. (1987b) 'A topographical commentary on the coin finds from ninth century Northumbria', in Metcalf 1987a, pp. 361–82.

Mills, D. (1976) *The Place-Names of Lancashire*, Batsford.

Morgan, P. (1978) *Great Domesday Book, Cheshire*, Phillimore.

Morris, J. (1973, rev. 1975) *The Age of Arthur. A History of the British Isles from 350–650*, Weidenfeld & Nicolson.

Bibliography

Morris, M. (ed.) (1983) *The Archaeology of Greater Manchester, 1, Medieval Manchester*, Greater Manchester Archaeological Unit.
Nicholaisen, W. F. H. (1982) 'Old European names in Britain', *Nomina*, **6**, 37–42.
Nitz, H-J. (1988) 'Settlement structure and settlement systems of the Frankish central state in Carolingian and Ottonian times', in Hooke 1988, pp. 249–74.
Oldfield, F. & Statham, D. C. (1963) 'Pollen analytical data from Urswick tarn and Ellerside Moss, North Lancashire', *New Phytologist*, **62**, 53–66.
Oldfield, F. & Statham, D. C. (1965) 'Stratigraphy and pollen analysis on Cockerham and Pilling Mosses in North Lancashire', *Manchester Lit. & Phil.*, **107**, 70–85.
Oliver, A. (1982) 'The Ribchester *vicus* and its context – the results of recent excavations', in *Rural Settlement in the Roman North*, ed. P. Clack and S. Haselgrove, University of Durham Department of Archaeology, pp. 133–47.
Page, R. I. (1971) 'How long did the Scandinavian language survive in England? The epigraphical evidence', in *England before the Conquest: Studies in Primary Sources presented to Dorothy Whitelock*, ed. P. Clemoes and K. Hughes, Cambridge University Press, pp. 165–81.
Pennington, W. (1970) 'Vegetational history in the north west of England, a regional study', in *Studies in the Vegetational History of the British Isles*, ed. D. Walker and R. West, Cambridge University Press, pp. 41–80.
Piggott, C. D. & Huntley, J. P. (1978) 'Factors controlling the distribution of *Tilia cordata* at the northern limits of its geographical range, I, Distribution in North-West England', *New Phytologist*, **81**, 429–41.
Piggott, C. D. & Huntley, J. P. (1980) 'Factors controlling the distribution of *Tilia cordata* at the northern limits of its geographical range, II, History in North-West England', *New Phytologist*, **84**, 145–64.
Piggott, C. D. & Huntley, J. P. (1981) 'Factors controlling the distribution of *Tilia cordata* at the northern limits of its geographical range, III, Nature and causes of seed sterility', *New Phytologist*, **87**, 817–29.
Piggott, S. (1958) 'Native economics and the Roman occupation of North Britain', in Richmond, pp. 1–27.
Pirie, E. J. E. (1987) 'Phases and groups within the *styca* coinage of Northumbria', in Metcalf 1987a, pp. 103–46.
Potter, T. (1979a) *Romans in North West England*, Titus Wilson (Kendal).
Potter, T. (1979b) 'Heysham Excavations, summary', *Report of the Sixth Annual Archaeological Conference*, University of Lancaster, 8–9.
Powell, T. G. E. *et al.* (1963) 'Excavations at Skelmore Heads near Ulverston, 1957 and 1959', *CW*, ns, **63**, 1–30.
Prince, S. D. (1976) 'The effect of climate on grain development in barley at an upland site', *New Phytologist*, **76**, 377–89.
Rackham, O. (1976) *Trees and Woodland in the British Landscape*, Dent.
Richmond, I. A. (ed.) (1958) *Roman and Native in North Britain*, Nelson.

Rodgers, H. B. (1955) 'Land-use in Tudor Lancashire: the evidence of the Final Concords', *Inst. Brit. Geographers*, **21**, 79–97.

Rollinson, W. (1963) 'The lost villages and hamlets of Low Furness', *CW*, ns, **63**, 160–9.

Rollinson, W. (1967) *A History of Man in the Lake District*, Dent.

Ross, A. & Robins, D. (1989) *The Life and Death of a Druid Prince*, Rider.

Salway, P. (1981, rev. 1982) *The Oxford History of England, I, Roman Britain*, Oxford University Press.

Sawyer, P. H. (1971) *The Age of the Vikings*, Edward Arnold.

Sawyer, P. H. (ed.) (1976) *Medieval Settlement*, Edward Arnold.

Sawyer, P. H. (1978) *From Roman Britain to Norman England*, Methuen.

Sawyer, P. H. (1983) 'The royal **tūn** in pre-Conquest England', in *Ideal and Reality in Frankish and Anglo-Saxon Society*, ed. P. Wormald, D. Bullough and R. Collins, Blackwell, pp. 273–99.

Scofield, R. S. (1965) 'The geographical distribution of wealth in England 1334–1649', *Economic History Review*, 2nd ser., **18**, 483–510.

Selkirk, A. (1978) 'Ribblehead', *Current Archaeology*, **61**, 38–41.

Shaw, R. C. (1956) *The Royal Forest of Lancaster*, Guardian Press (Preston).

Shaw, R. C. (1963) *Post-Roman Carlisle and the Kingdoms of the North West*, Guardian Press (Preston).

Shotter, D. C. A. (1984) *Roman North West England*, Centre for North-West Regional Studies, Lancaster University, Occasional Paper, 14.

Simmons I. G. & Tooley, M. J. (1981) *The Environment of British Prehistory*, Duckworth.

Smith, A. G. (1958) 'Two lacustrine deposits in the south of the English Lake District', *New Phytologist*, **57**, 363–86.

Smith, A. G. (1959) 'The meres of south west Westmorland: stratigraphy and pollen analysis', *New Phytologist*, **58**, 105–27.

Smith, A. H. (1956) *English Place-Name Elements*, English Place-Name Society, 25, 26.

Smith, L. P. (1976) *The Agricultural Climate of England and Wales*, Ministry of Agriculture, Food and Fisheries Technical Bulletin, 35.

Smith, R. B. (1961) *Blackburnshire. A Study in Early Lancashire History*, Leicester University Department of English Local History Occasional Paper, 15.

Smith, W. (1941) *Lancashire*, Land Utilization Survey, 45.

Sobee, F. J. (1953) *A History of Pilling* (privately printed).

Somerville, R. (1953) *History of the Duchy of Lancaster, I, 1265–1603*, Chancellor and Council of the Duchy of Lancaster.

Stamp, L. D. (ed.) (1962) *The Land of Britain*, Report of the Land Utilization Survey of Britain.

Stead, I. M. *et al.* (1986) *Lindow Man, The Body in the Bog*, British Museum.

Tait, J. (1904) *Medieval Manchester and the Beginnings of Lancashire*, Manchester University Press.

Tallis, J. H. (1964) 'Studies on Southern Pennine peats', *Jnl Ecology*, **52**, 323–53.

Tallis, J. H. & McGuire, J. (1972) 'Central Rossendale: the evolution of an upland vegetation, I, the clearance of woodland', *Jnl Ecology*, **60**, 721–37.

Taylor, C. C. (1983) *Village and Farmstead*, George Philip.

Thomas, C. (1971) *The Early Christian Archaeology of North Britain*, Oxford University Press.

Tooley, M. J. (1978) *Sea Level Changes in North West England During the Flandrian Stage*, Clarendon Press.

Turnbull, P. (1984) 'Stanwick in the Northern Iron Age', *Durham Archaeol. Jnl*, **1**, 41–9.

Turnbull, P. & Fitts, L. (1988) 'The politics of Brigantia', in *Recent Research in Roman Yorkshire, Studies in Honour of Mary Kitson Clark (Mrs Derwas Chitty)*, BAR Brit. Ser., 193, pp. 377–86.

Wainwright, F. T. (1945–46) 'The Scandinavians in Lancashire', *LCAS*, **58**, 71–116.

Wainwright, F. T. *et al.* (no date) Unpublished collection of field-names in the Lancashire Record Office.

Walker, J. S. F. (ed.) (1986) *The Archaeology of Greater Manchester, 3, Roman Manchester, a Frontier Settlement*, Greater Manchester Archaeological Unit.

Waterhouse, J. (1985) *The Stone Circles of Cumbria*, Phillimore.

Webb, A. N. (ed.) (1970) *The Cartulary of Burscough Priory*, CS, 3rd ser, 18.

Weinriech, U. (1963) *Languages in Contact: Findings and Problems*, Mouton (The Hague).

Wheeler, R. E. M. (1954) *The Stanwick Fortifications*, Society of Antiquaries Research Report, 17.

Whitelock, D. (ed.) (1955) *English Historical Documents, I, c. 500–1042*, Eyre & Spottiswoode.

Whittock, M. J. (1986) *The Origins of England 410–600*, Croom Helm.

Winchester, A. (1987) *Landscape and Society in Medieval Cumbria*, John Donald.

Young, C. R. (1979) *The Royal Forests of Medieval England*, Leicester University Press.

Index

Index

Barrow-in-Furness, 86
Barton (Amounderness), 91 fig. 4.3, 106
Barton (Salford hundred), 106–7, 180 fig. 4.7, 117
Barton (West Derby hundred), 6
Barwick in Elmet, 71
Beca Bank, 78
Bede, 65, 76–8
Bedfordshire, 114
Beetham, 159–60
Bellême (Robert de), 156
Bentham, 159–60
Berkshire, 90
Bernicia, 63, 77
Billinge, 2, 6, 82, 84
Billington, 82
Birkby, 89, 141
Birkdale, 3, 133
Birkrigg Common, 23, 32
Bispham (Amounderness), 13, 82, 90, 91 fig. 4.3, 92, 144–6
Bispham (Leyland hundred), 73, 82, 90
Black Lake (Pilling), 9
Blackburn, 20 fig. 1.4, 81–2, 85, 90, 99, 100, 101 fig. 2.6, 141–2, 162, 172, 180
Blackburn hundred, 85, 89, 95, 96 fig. 4.5, 99, 101 fig. 4.6, 103, 105, 115, 116 fig. 5.1, 141–2, 153, 162, 166, 169
Blackburnshire (Chase of), 172
Blackley, 107
Blackpool, 5, 6, 8, 10, 13
Blackrod, 79
Blatchinworth, 107
Bleasdale, 27, 92
Bolingbroke (Henry of), 21, 176, 178
Bolrun (William de), 168
Bolton (near Urswick), 106
Bolton-le-Moors, 11, 106–7, 108 fig. 4.7, 137, 166, 173 fig. 6.7
Bolton-le-Sands, 93 fig. 4.4, 124, 136, 147, 172
Borrowdale, 3
Borwick, 107, 160

Botler (alias Butler, q.v.), 163
Boudicca, 46
Boulogne, 156
Bowerham, 168
Bowland, 1, 5, 6, 11, 14, 27, 104, 147, 172
Brantwood, 105
Brathay, 157
Bridgewater (Duke of), 9
Briercliffe, 35
Brigantes, 24, 38–40, 45–6, 50–1, 78
Brigantia, 24, 38–9, 46–8, 51, 53
Britannia Inferior, 51, 59
Britannia Secunda, 78
Britannia Superior, 51, 59
Broadfleet, 60
Bryning, 82
Brynn, 71, 86
Burn, 82
Burnage, 82
Burnley, 35, 36, 82, 102, 162
Burrow Heights (near Lancaster), 57
Burrow in Lonsdale, 20 fig. 1.4, 48, 49 fig. 2.5, 58
Burscough, 9, 10, 22
Bury, 37, 166, 173 fig. 6.7
Busli, 156
Bussel, 156, 159–60, 161 fig. 6.6, 163
Butler, 161 fig. 6.6, 163–4
  Richard de, 163
Butterworth, 137

Caer Gybi, 59
Calder Fell, 2
Calder, 2, 3, 4 fig. 1.2, 34–5, 41 fig. 2.3, 84, 100, 141, 162
Calder (tributary of Wyre), 3
Calderstones, 27
Cambridge, 41
Camp Fell (near Liverpool), 37
Camulodunum, 46
Cantsfield, 82, 85, 136
Caratacus, 46
Carlegion (alias Chester, q.v.), 65
Carleton, 91 fig. 4.3, 106, 133

Index

Index

Foulridge, 102
France, 155
Freckleton, 106, 168
Frontinus, 48
Fulwood, 68, 91 fig. 4.3, 170
Furness, 1–3, 5–6, 13–14, 17, 20
 fig. 1.4, 23, 30, 32, 42, 50, 52, 74,
 105, 113, 123–4, 127, 130, 136,
 141, 147, 148, 153–4, 156–7,
 160, 161 fig. 6.6, 162, 168, 172,
 174
Fylde, 3, 6, 8–12, 17, 21–2, 27, 40,
 54, 58, 71, 73, 79, 84–6, 90, 92,
 94, 99, 106, 115–16, 124, 129,
 130, 133, 135, 138, 141, 144, 145
 fig. 6.2, 146–7, 152, 163, 168

Gamel (patron of Pennington
 Church, North Lancashire), 129,
 174
Gamel of Rochdale, 143 fig. 6.1,
 144, 151, 155, 166, 172
Gargrave, 53
Garstang, 13, 20 fig. 1.4, 36, 40, 92,
 134–5, 144, 145 fig. 6.2, 146–7,
 160, 161 fig. 6.6, 167–9
Gaunt (John of), 177
Gawthwaite, 23
Genouii, 51
Germany, 39
Gernet, 168, 170
Glodwick, 71
Glossop, 18
Godley Lane, 102
Golbourne, 82
Goosnargh, 136, 145 fig. 6.2, 147,
 174
Gospatric, 153
Grange-Over-Sands, 3
Greece, 51
Grelley, 143 fig. 6.1, 156, 161 fig.
 6.6, 166
 Albert (fl. 1086), 156, 166
 Albert (fl. 1154–62), 173–4
 Robert, 170
Greslet (alias Grelley, q.v.), 156
Gresli (alias Grelley, q.v.), 166
Gressingham, 82, 84, 92, 93 fig.

4.4, 102, 121, 165
Greta, 33, 42, 98
Grimston, 35
Grindleton, 153
Gwynedd, 77

Habergham, 82, 84
Hackinsall, 129, 134
Hakirke, 112
Halfdan, 110
Hallamshire, 100
Halsall, 9, 63
Halton (Cheshire), 20 fig. 1.4, 155,
 164, 176
Halton (Lancashire), 20 fig. 1.4,
 58, 93, 102, 109, 121, 122 fig. 5.4,
 147, 153–4, 167–8, 170, 172
Hamwih, 98
Hardknott, 49 fig. 2.5, 50
Haskayne, 6, 71
Hastings, 82
Hasty Knoll, 79–80
Haume, 147
Hawkshead, 3, 11, 135–6, 157, 158
 fig. 6.5
Haworth, 107
Hawsclough (Clayton-le-Woods),
 37
Heaton (with Oxcliffe), 93 fig. 6.4
Heaton Norris, 166
Helewise de Lancaster, 160
Helmshore, 14
Henry Bolingbroke (also known as
 Henry of Lancaster, and Henry
 IV), 21–2, 178
Henry I, 153, 156–7, 166
Henry II, 152, 159, 165, 167, 170
Henry III, 170, 175
Henry (son of David of Scotland),
 157
Henry (son of Siward), 173
Henry de Lacy, 176
Henry 4th Earl of Lancaster, 177
Hesketh, 133
Hesketh Bank, 7
Hesketh-Fleetwood (Sir Peter), 65
Heslerton, 97
Hest (Bank), 92, 93 fig. 4.4

Stalybridge, 138
Stephen (king of England), 154,
  156–8, 160, 164–6
Stone Close (Stainton), 32
Stockport, 79, 99
Strathclyde, 23, 112–13, 123, 130
Suffolk, 159
Sunderland, 13
Swainset (alias Swainshead), 128,
  144
Swainshead, 128, 144, 170
Swale, 46
Swinside, 32

Tacitus, 38, 46, 48
Taillebois (Ivo de), 160
Tatham, 82, 84, 87, 98, 103, 159,
  160
Tectoverdi, 39
Tees, 46, 151
Teyrnllwg, 71
Thames, 15
Thelwall, 18, 20 fig. 1.4, 62, 112,
  117, 163
Theodore, 78
Thingwall, 132
Thirnby, 149
Thomas (de Walton), 168
Thornham, 82, 84
Thornton (Amounderness), 144
Thornton (West Derby hundred), 6
Thornton (Yorkshire), 159
Threlfall, 144
Thuri, 127
Thurstan, 157
Tickhill, 156
Tosti, 58, 116, 121, 123, 140–1,
  144, 148–9, 152–3, 167
Tottington, 165–6, 172
Trawden, 11, 35
Treales, 20 fig. 1.4, 62, 68, 91–2,
  94, 144
Trent, 77–9, 170
Trough of Bowland, 5
Tulketh, 68, 156
Tunstall, 159
Turton, 127

Tutbury, 176
Tweed, 153–4
Tyldesley, 68, 104, 164
Tyne, 40

Uhtred, 105, 132, 142–3, 151, 164
Ulf, 141, 159
Ulnes Walton, 71, 89
Ulverston, 17, 23, 27, 30, 106, 110,
  157, 158 fig. 6.5, 174
Upbrook Farm (near Clitheroe),
  35
Urien of Rheged, 70
Urm, 173
Urmston, 106
Urswick, 23, 33, 42, 102, 156–7,
  158 fig. 6.5, 174
Urswick Tarn, 30

Valens, 59
Valentia, 59
Valentinian, 59
Venutius, 47–8
Villers (Pain de), 164
Virconium, 23

Wadden Thorpe, 14
Wakefield, 137
Wales, 18, 48, 84, 94, 129, 165,
  176, 178
Wallasey, 164
Wallingford, 158
Walmersley, 37–8
Walney Island, 7, 14, 4 fig. 1.2, 29
  fig. 2.1, 31 fig. 2.2, 32–3, 82
Walsden, 89, 108 fig. 4.7
Walsden Gorge, 5
Walton, 56–7, 71, 89, 110–11, 115,
  143,
Walton-le-Dale, 18, 20 fig. 1.4, 48,
  49 fig. 2.5, 55–7, 61–2, 73, 84,
  89–90, 115, 116 fig. 5.1, 142, 169
Walton-on-the-Hill, 63, 142
Warbreck, 129, 133, 146
Wardleworth, 107, 137
Warenne (William de, also known

Index